THE S.A.S.D. BIDS FAREWELL TO WISE AND ANCIENT GUARDIAN

We are deeply saddened to report the death of the Guardian, chief among the members of the Society of Dragons. This esteemed, 850-year-old female European dragon, also known as the Wantley Dam, had been guarding the powerful gem known as the Dragon's Eye since 1281, as well as many other treasures of the S.A.S.D. She was known for her strong relationships with human Dragon Masters through the ages, helping to maintain peace between human- and dragon-kind. Mysterious circumstances surround her death: it is claimed by reputable sources that she was cruelly slain by Russian self-proclaimed 'dragonologist' Alexandra Goryntchka, who has since disappeared. She is thought to have taken with her two stolen treasures of the S.A.S.D: Splatterfax — the war amulet of the Viking Rus, and the Spear of Saint George. Ignatius Crook, son of former Dragon Master Ebenezer Crook, was also implicated in the Guardian's death. He is missing, presumed dead. Also missing is Saint Gilbert's Horn, another of the S.A.S.D.'s treasures, stolen from the Guardian by Crook. The Society of Dragons is still to decide on a suitable candidate to replace their indomitable leader.

NEW DRAGON MASTER IS CONFIRMED!

On a brighter note, before the sad death of the Guardian she used her flame to burn the image of the renowned dragonologist Dr. Ernest Drake into the Dragon's Eye gem, confirming him as the new Dragon Master. After the death of the previous Dragon Master, Ebenezer Crook, in 1875, nobody suitable had been found to take on this role, which bears the weighty responsibility of being mankind's sole representative to the British Society of Dragons. Many members of the S.A.S.D. will doubtless have encountered Dr. Drake on visits to the well-loved shop, Dr. Drake's Dragonalia, on Wyvern Way, London. Members may also have heard of Dr. Drake's dragonology school, which he runs from his home, Castle Drake, in St. Leonard's Forest, Horsham. The S.A.S.D. would like to congratulate Dr. Drake not only on his well-deserved confirmation as Dragon Master, but also on his endeavours this summer, aided by his young apprentices Daniel and Beatrice Cook. This brave trio together managed to prevent the treasured Dragon's Eye gem from falling into dangerous hands. Mr. and Mrs. John Cook, the parents of Daniel and Beatrice and two of Dr. Drake's closest friends, will shortly be returning from their dragonological works in India to congratulate the new Dragon Master in person. The S.A.S.D. wishes Dr. Drake much good fortune in his future work.

FOR A FULL ACCOUNT OF THESE EVENTS, READ *THE DRAGON'S EYE: VOLUME I* of THE DRAGONOLOGY CHRONICLES

CONTENTS

LIST OF ILLUSTRATIONS

LIST OF ILLUSTRATIONS

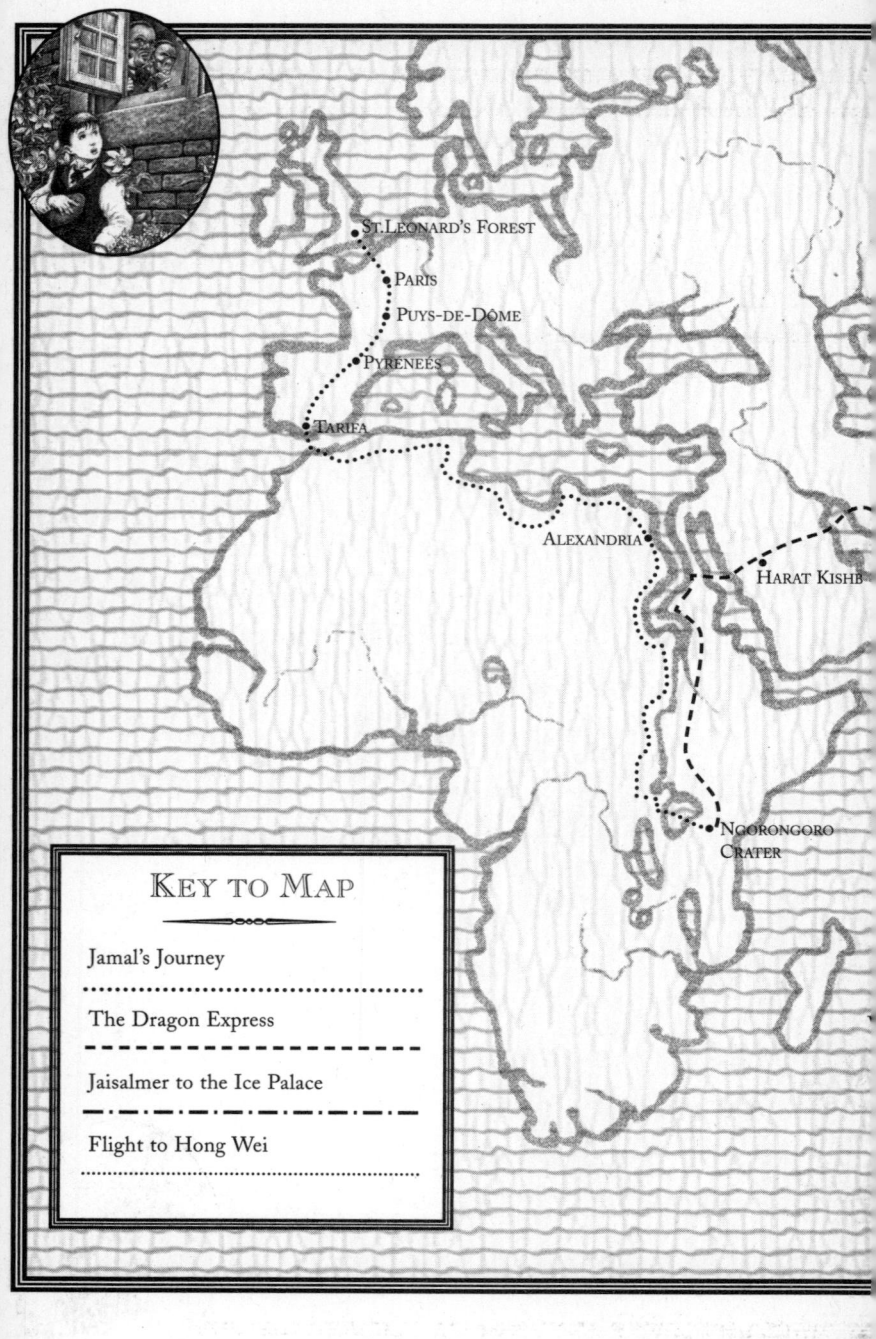

ST. LEONARD'S FOREST

PARIS

PUYS-DE-DÔME

PYRENEES

TARIFA

ALEXANDRIA

HARAT KISHB

NGORONGORO CRATER

KEY TO MAP

Jamal's Journey

....

The Dragon Express

– – – – – – – – – – – –

Jaisalmer to the Ice Palace

–·–·–·–·–·–·–·–·–·–·

Flight to Hong Wei

....

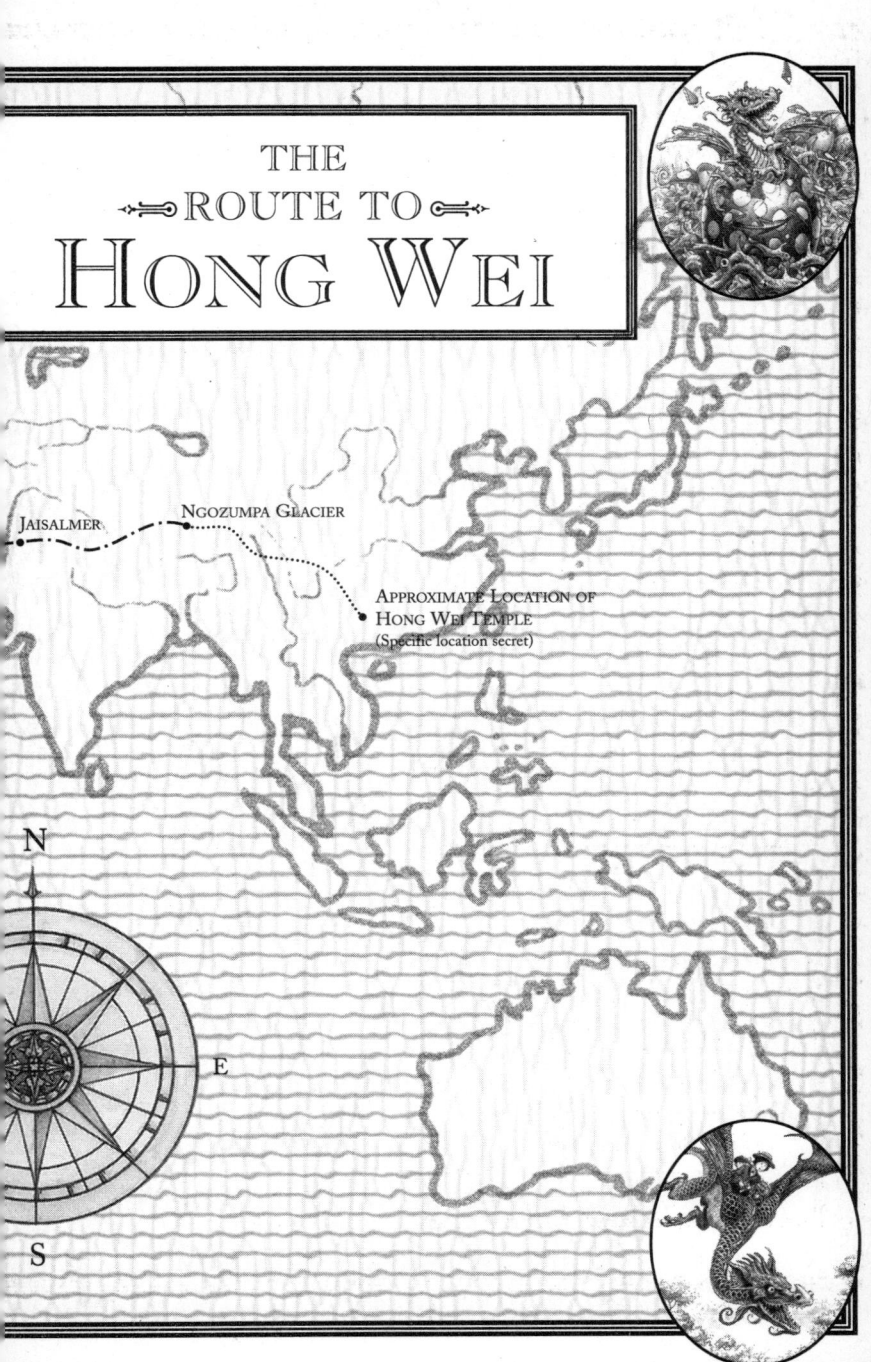

THE
⟻ ROUTE TO ⟼
HONG WEI

JAISALMER

NGOZUMPA GLACIER

APPROXIMATE LOCATION OF
HONG WEI TEMPLE
(Specific location secret)

N

E

S

PROLOGUE

Beyond the dunes, beyond the scrub, three red sunsets and three orange dawns out of the city of Jaisalmer, far away across the Thar Desert, the vultures wheeled high in the air. A man sat back on his camel and looked up at them. He drew his hand across his face to shade it, peering into the sun to watch the vultures dive, then flap upwards again with agitated, frustrated movements. A hot wind had been blowing from the east all day. Now a sudden change in its direction made his camel start. It flared its nostrils and looked around. The man patted its neck and spoke to it soothingly. But his face, under his slouch hat, looked grim. He set off again.

It wasn't long before the man spotted the first carcass. Sand was already starting to cover it. The man climbed down from his camel and covered the last hundred yards on foot. He saw that what had looked like eight small dunes were, in fact, eight more carcasses, all half-covered with sand. The smallest carcass was about eight feet long; the largest, over forty, its scaly bulk disappearing underground. Along the length of their bodies, the creatures were like snakes. But at the top end, each looked almost human, with a torso, a head and two arms. On closer inspection, it was clear that they were not human at all. They were dead nagas.

The man bent down to examine the smallest naga more closely. It was still only a baby. Dried yellow spittle trailed from its mouth. The man frowned. He put down his pack and took out a notebook and a small bag. Then he unclasped a pocketknife and reached down to take a small sample of the spittle on the blade. Being as careful as possible, he lifted the knife up towards him very, very slowly until...

A rifle cocked behind his ear. The man froze.

A cockney voice said, "Give 'em a break, mate. They're dead." The man turned around slowly to face his assailant.

The cockney, who was wearing a dirty black jacket that was streaked white with desert dust, grinned at him with yellow teeth.

"You're Noah Hayes," he said. "I know your name. And I know your game, too. You can call me Shadwell."

The man put away his pocketknife, then took off his hat and used it to wipe his brow. He put it back on his head and spat on the ground.

"You're *Shadwell?*" he said, speaking in a Texan drawl. "I've heard you're a dealer in dragons. That is one *ugly* profession. What do you want from me, Shadwell?"

"If you're so interested in dead dragons and all, maybe you'd like to see a live one," replied Shadwell, grinning again.

Keeping his gun pointed at Noah Hayes with his right hand, Shadwell unbuttoned his jacket with his left. As he did so, a puff of smoke came out of the inside pocket, and a small, scaly creature climbed out and looked at Hayes with hard, beady eyes. It was a dwarf dragon.

"Say hello to Flitz," said Shadwell.

The dragon peered around and bared his teeth at Hayes. But as soon as he saw the dead naga, he recoiled and looked very much as though he would rather climb back into the safety of Shadwell's jacket pocket.

Seeing Flitz's discomfort, Shadwell gave a harsh laugh.

"That's right, Flitz," he said. "The poor nagas all got sick and died. But don't worry. You don't have to touch them. We've got some kidnapping to do instead."

Shadwell gestured towards Hayes. Flitz turned to fix his eyes on the Texan. Then, not looking away from him for a moment, the dragon climbed up onto Shadwell's shoulder. Shadwell didn't move, and he kept his rifle aimed at Hayes.

"Go get him, boy," he said.

At Shadwell's command, Flitz flew straight at Noah Hayes with his claws outstretched and his fangs bared, at the ready.

Hayes screamed and tried to cover his face. Just as he did so, out from behind a dune stepped the most sinister-looking woman he had ever seen...

Chapter I
The Egg

Dragons cannot help but find the sounds humans produce, when they
attempt to speak Dragonish for the first time, incomprehensible,
no matter how much they roar, gurgle or hiss.
—Liber Draconis, 'First Wintermoon'

Looking out of the classroom through the rain,
I noticed that Dr. Drake's garden seemed strangely
empty. Usually there were birds sheltering in the branches
of the magnolia tree, but today there were none to be
seen, and instead I watched a single fat rabbit hop out of
the beech forest and onto the lawn. Inside the classroom,
Dr. Drake himself was standing in front of the small
blackboard, teaching us the rudiments of dragon grammar.

My sister, Beatrice, and I had been enrolled in
Dr. Drake's school some months earlier and had already
learned a great deal about dragons and the little-known
science of dragonology. We would have learned more had
our studies not been interrupted by all manner of

adventures, albeit ones instructive in themselves as far as learning about the ways of dragons was concerned. In comparison, being back in the classroom was a bit of a bore, though normally I would have been fascinated by Dr. Drake's lessons. The trouble was that for nearly three weeks we had spent every day inside because of incessant downpours. Now all I wanted to do was to head out into the forest and study a real dragon again.

I looked back out across the lawn. Suddenly, the rabbit looked up. It paused, and then it was gone, streaking away behind a flower bed and into the orchard. At the edge of the forest, the leaves of the magnolia had begun shaking wildly.

Jamal! I thought.

I leaned sideways in my chair, trying to catch a glimpse of the playful wyvern that Dr. Drake was taking care of until he was old enough to be returned to his native home in Africa. But instead of Jamal, I spotted a long, leathery, snakelike body scurrying down out of the tree and slithering away into the ferns beyond. It was only Weasel, a knucker dragon that lived in the forest near Castle Drake. No doubt she had been out hunting rabbits and had been using the tree for cover.

But the tree continued to shake, and I decided that

there was a good chance that Jamal was there as well. I turned to tell Dr. Drake, but then I realised that he was already talking to me. I only managed to catch the end of what he said, which had something to do with stopping daydreaming and concentrating on the job at hand. Beatrice, who was sitting at the next desk, glared at me.

"Er, I'm very sorry, Dr. Drake," I said. "But—"

"Forget the forest for once, Daniel!" said Dr. Drake. "You are no longer a mere Dragonological Apprentice. As an Alumnus, you will do much better in your studies once you can speak Dragonish. And you won't be able to speak any Dragonish if you can't conjugate verbs."

"But Jamal has—"

"Never mind Jamal!" he cried. "Mademoiselle Gamay is looking after him, and I am sure she is doing an excellent job."

Dr. Drake turned back to the blackboard.

"Now!" he said. "The verb meaning 'to fly'. It is a regular verb, like all verbs in Dragonish. Who can remember what it is — Daniel?"

My mind went blank. I had been terrible at languages at boarding school, and this was no different. This wasn't dragonology — it was torture! Out of the corner of my eye, I could see that the tree had stopped shaking.

Where had Jamal gone now?

I looked down at my desk and could feel Dr. Drake looking at me, waiting for my answer. Any chance that I might ever grow up to be a Dragonologist First Class, let alone a Dragon Master like Dr. Drake, was slipping further and further away.

"Beatrice?" said Dr. Drake at last.

"*Algrrrrai*, sir," said Beatrice, giving the *r* in the middle what I felt to be a deliberately annoying roll.

"Good," said Dr. Drake. "*Algrai*, 'to fly'. The command form, 'Fly!' Darcy?"

"The same," said Darcy. "*Algrai.*"

"Good. 'I fly'. Beatrice?"

"*Algroo.*"

"'You fly'?"

"*Algrow.*"

"You see, Daniel," said Dr. Drake. "It has the same form as the verb we learned yesterday, 'to see'. *Ivàhsi, ivàhsoo, ivàhsow, ivàhsi, ivàhsumble, ivàhsumple, ivàhsarch!*"

"Yes, sir." I said.

"So can you conjugate *algrai*, Daniel?"

I fiddled nervously in my pocket, where I kept my most prized possessions: a piece of flint and a piece of iron pyrites. The last time we had managed to do some dragonological fieldwork, Darcy, a fellow student who was staying at Castle Drake like ourselves, had given Beatrice and me a set each. He had shown us how dragons use these stones to make the sparks that light the flammable venom in their mouths. But my knowledge of how dragons produce fire was not going to help me in my current predicament.

"Daniel?" said Dr. Drake.

"*Algrai, algroo, algrow, algri, algrumble, algrumple, al — er —*"

"*Algrarch!*" said Dr. Drake. "But of course, it's not like an *r*. It's more like a..."

"Like a what, sir?" I said.

"You have to roll your *r*s, Daniel, like a dragon. Like this! Like—"

But just at that moment, a deafening roar from outside the classroom drowned out Dr. Drake's voice. The walls shook. Darcy, Beatrice, and I all turned around to look out through the window at the back of the classroom and saw a large but very familiar dragon's head pressed sideways up to the glass, staring in at us with one eye.

"Oh!" cried Beatrice. "It's Jamal! Jamal has come to visit us!"

"PRRRRAISICH HOYARRRRI!" roared the adolescent wyvern in greeting.

"That's the way to do it!" shouted Darcy. "That's the way to roll your *r*s!"

We all laughed, including Dr. Drake, who laughed so hard that he actually had to take off his flat cap and mop his brow with it.

Jamal bobbed up and down like a gigantic plucked turkey right outside the window as the rain bounced off his scales. And there, behind him, was Mademoiselle Gamay, holding a torn umbrella in one hand and lifting up her long, damp skirt with the other as she dashed across the lawn.

"Oh, dear," said Dr. Drake. "I believe that Mademoiselle Gamay needs a spot of help, after all."

By now Mademoiselle Gamay had dodged inside the door and was shaking the broken umbrella frantically.

"I am so sorry, Ernest," she said. "Jamal is very nearly ready to fly, and I just could not keep him at the compound. He has been missing the children, I think."

"I expect that he has, Dominique," said Dr. Drake. "But we had better take him back straight away. We must not encourage him to keep escaping. I shall come and help."

"Can we help, too?" I asked.

Dr. Drake looked thoughtful for a moment.

"Darcy can help," he said. "But I think that you two ought to go and check up on the egg. It should be ready to hatch any day now."

Normally I would have been happy to do as he asked, for it wasn't any ordinary egg we were looking after. It was the egg of a European dragon; Dr. Drake had put us in charge of it until it hatched. But I did long to go outside.

My face must have grown longer, since Dr. Drake added just as he left, "Cheer up, Daniel! It can't rain forever. By my estimate, your parents ought to have reached Suez by now. The dragon chick is sure to hatch before they come home. I dare say you and Beatrice are rather looking forward to showing them how well you've been doing with it!"

Dr. Drake was right. I *was* looking forward to it, very much. I hadn't seen my parents for four years, since they had travelled to the mysterious Indian city of Jaisalmer to work for the city's ruler, the Maharawal, as dragonological investigators. They had been engaged on an urgent mission among the nagas of the Thar Desert, but now, at last, they were coming home.

Beatrice and I picked up our dragonological record

books — in which we wrote down anything we learned about dragons — and, huddling together under a black tarpaulin, we splashed our way along the garden path to the old coal shed, where we had prepared a lair for the new dragon chick. We had collected a large pile of shiny objects to use as a nest and had laid out next to it the long tongs that we used to turn the egg, as well as the heavy sledgehammer that we would need to crack it when the time came. The egg itself was lying on a charcoal brazier to one side. It had been four weeks since Dr. Drake had been given the egg to look after by its injured mother, Scramasax, and each day we had watched its colour change very gradually, from a sort of ruddy brown to a bright purple.

"How long do you think it will take Mother and Father to get home?" I asked Beatrice when we had got inside.

"I don't know, Daniel," said Beatrice. "I suppose another couple of weeks."

"Will the chick have hatched by then, do you think?"

"Let's see," she said, and turned to look at a chart on the wall that showed how the colour of a European dragon's egg changed during the course of its incubation. Each week, we had made a mark on the chart after comparing our egg to it. Now there was hardly any difference between the colour of the egg before us and the shade of purple right at the end of the chart.

"It might hatch any day now," said Beatrice.

I picked up the tongs, lifted the egg to one side for a moment and piled more charcoal on the brazier.

※

I didn't have any hope at all that the weather would improve by the afternoon, and so it was no surprise to find myself back in the classroom after lunch. But instead of Dr. Drake, Mademoiselle Gamay, who had managed to dry out and change her clothes, was standing at the front of the class.

"I am afraid Dr. Drake has some important business to attend to," she said. "And so I shall be teaching this afternoon's class — on the city-dwelling dragon known as the gargouille."

This did not come as much of a surprise, either. Since he had become Dragon Master and the head of the Secret and Ancient Society of Dragonologists only a few weeks before, Dr. Drake had become increasingly busy.

"Perhaps he has heard news of Ignatius," I whispered anxiously to Beatrice. Ignatius Crook was Dr. Drake's sworn enemy and had nearly caused all three of us to be buried beneath a mountain earlier in the summer.

"Daniel," she hissed back, "as far as we know, Ignatius Crook is dead."

"Dr. Drake doesn't seem to think so," I replied. "He said it was quite likely that Ignatius escaped."

Before Beatrice could reply, Emery Cloth, a dragonologist friend of Dr. Drake's, came bursting into the classroom.

"So sorry to interrupt the class," he said. "But I need Beatrice and Daniel right now! Dr. Drake says to come at once! The tapping noises have begun!"

Soon we were all crowded into the coal shed along with Dr. Drake and Emery. Beatrice and I stepped to the front by the charcoal brazier.

Tap, went the dragon chick, hitting the inside of the shell with its egg tooth as it tried to crack it.

Tap! Tap!
TAP! TAP! TAP!

The egg was rocking backwards and forwards in the flames.

Tap! Tap! Tap!
TAP! TAP! TAP! TAP! TAP!

"Right, Daniel," said Dr. Drake. "Take hold of the egg with those tongs, as I showed you. You needn't be gentle, and you must *not* be slow."

I quickly picked up the long pair of tongs, reached over the flames and grasped the egg. I could feel the heat travelling up the iron handles from the fire. The egg was heavy, but I had expected that. I lifted it up and placed it on the stone floor.

The tapping grew even louder, and the egg began to roll about wildly.

"Well done," said Dr. Drake. "Now, Beatrice, do you think you can manage the sledgehammer?"

"I think so," said Beatrice. But she looked very small as she took the handle of the heavy sledgehammer and raised it over her head.

"Wait until the egg has stopped moving," said Dr. Drake.

Beatrice waited, the head of the sledgehammer tottering above her. I moved out of the way.

"Now!" he said.

SMASH! Beatrice brought the sledgehammer down on top of the egg as hard as she could. It did not seem to have made an impression, but the tapping inside stopped.

"Again!" cried Dr. Drake.

SMASH! Beatrice brought the hammer down again. And *SMASH!* And *SMASH!* And...

"Stop!" cried Dr. Drake.

Beatrice just managed to stop herself.

A patina of cracks formed across the top of the egg. I stepped forward eagerly.

"Wait, Daniel," commanded Dr. Drake. "The egg is still red-hot!"

We waited. The tapping started again.

Tap! Tap! Tap!

TAP! TAP!...

Suddenly, a piece of shell from the top of the egg dropped off and fell onto the floor. Then another piece followed it, and another. A dragon's snout with a tiny horn struck upwards out of the shell. A head emerged, followed by a thin neck and a scraggy, red, scaly body, two sharp little claws, and two folded-up little wings. A tail with a large arrowhead at the end flicked out. The chick fixed us with its beady eyes. It sneezed twice in a jerky motion, and a lot of green, phlegmy stuff came out of its mouth and nose. Then it looked up at us, gave a faint little roar and stretched out its tiny wings for the first time.

"Ooooh!" said Beatrice. "It's a boy! Isn't he adorable?"

"Ooooh!" said Beatrice. "It's a boy! Isn't he adorable?"

Chapter II
THE NEW ARRIVAL

An instinct to play is among the foremost desires of all young creatures.
— Liber Draconis, 'The Humanology Handbook'

The moment the chick had hatched, while we were still oohing and aahing, Dr. Drake lifted his gold pocket watch from his waistcoat and made a note in Beatrice's record book of the time he was born.

"Seventeen minutes past one," he said. "Now, if you others wouldn't mind leaving us, it is time for Daniel and Beatrice to give this little fellow his bath."

Earlier in the week, Dr. Drake had explained that the first thing we needed to do after the chick hatched was to wash him, in order to cool him down and to clean the egg slime off him. Until the chick had been washed or, as Dr. Drake phrased it, 'dunked', we mustn't touch him, as he would still be nearly as hot as the scorching embers the egg had lain in.

I had volunteered for the task of bathing the chick,

and so I pulled on a pair of knobbly flame-resistant gloves, made from shed dragon skin, while Beatrice took an old green towel from the top of a pail of water that we had prepared. Then she knelt down in front of the chick while I stepped around behind him.

"Right, Daniel," said Dr. Drake. "Be quick."

I leaned forward and grasped the chick firmly with both hands. He did not like me taking hold of him and let out an angry roar, struggling hard as he tried to break free. There was a strong, sulphurous dragon smell coming off him, and he was surprisingly heavy. I had to grip his scales tightly in order to hold on to him. I could feel the heat of his wriggling, lizard-like body even through the thick gloves, and I had to hold my head back so that his wing tips didn't scratch me in the face. I dunked him straight down into the bucket of water. There was a loud hiss as the water came into contact with the chick's scales, and I found myself temporarily blinded by a cloud of steam. As soon as the chick was in the water, I let him go. The dunking bucket was on a set of scales, and Beatrice quickly read off the weight they registered.

"Twenty-one pounds, six ounces," she said.

"How heavy does that make the chick?" asked Dr. Drake.

"Well, the pail of water weighs nine pounds, so the chick's weight is twelve pounds six," she replied.

"Excellent," said Dr. Drake, jotting down the figure alongside the time of birth. "A very healthy weight. Now lift him out."

I groped for the chick in the steaming water. When he tried to nip me, I was glad that the gloves were bite-resistant. I soon got hold of him again, then hoisted him out and passed him to Beatrice, who had a towel open, ready to receive him. Once he was in the towel, the chick sneezed, wriggling and rubbing himself vigorously and giving me a very sulky look. Then Beatrice unwrapped the towel, and he leaped down nimbly. Whatever stiffness there had been in his limbs had vanished. Dashing between Dr. Drake's legs, he headed straight for the top of his new nest and began investigating the shiny objects we had put there for him, nudging some with his snout and lightly tapping others with his claws and tail. Then, rather clumsily, he began pulling some of the objects towards himself and pushing others away. He chose a necklace strung with artificial gems, a piece of broken mirror, the edges of which had been gently sanded to take the sharpness off them, a thick piece of steel chain, a small pewter tankard with coloured glass set around the top and a broken carriage clock of ornate design that had belonged to Dr. Drake. Once satisfied with his collection, he turned around and around like a dog before splaying out his legs and pressing his soft underbelly firmly onto the objects beneath him. Then he lifted his head back like a gigantic baby bird, opened his toothy jaws as wide as he could and began to make a high-pitched whining noise.

Almost on cue, there was a tap on the door and Darcy entered the coal shed, carrying a stockpot from the kitchen full of meaty kitchen scraps. The chick started sniffing loudly but did not move except to flick his dark-red forked tongue in and out.

Darcy put the pot down next to Beatrice, and she lifted off the lid.

"Daniel ought to feed him first," said Dr. Drake, "so that the chick forgives him for that bath."

Beatrice nodded, and I knelt down beside the nest.

"Don't forget the technique I showed you, Daniel!" said Dr. Drake. "Hold the palm of your hand completely flat with the food on top of it, as though you were feeding a horse."

I took some chicken meat and held it out to the chick.

But he ignored me, turning his head to look at Beatrice as though he hoped she was going to feed him.

Then suddenly he stood up, bared his teeth and roared at me.

I jumped backwards. The meat I had been holding out fell to the floor, and the chick dived towards it, grabbed it with his teeth and ran back to the top of his nest, where he devoured it in two quick gulps.

"You mustn't let him do that," said Beatrice.

"I couldn't help it," I said.

I tried again.

The chick looked hard at Beatrice and made a soft, guttural noise almost like a purr. Then he stood up and roared at me again. I only just managed to pull my hand out of the way as the chick lunged at the food, his long teeth snapping shut on the meat. I went to take another piece of food from the stockpot, but Dr. Drake, who was starting to look worried, waved me back.

"This part can be a little difficult," said Dr. Drake. "Dragon chicks don't like being dunked, even though it is necessary."

"I'm sure you'll get the hang of it soon, Daniel," said Beatrice.

"Why don't you try feeding him, then?" I said. "It's not that easy."

I moved out of the way, and Beatrice took some meat out of the stockpot. The dragon chick resumed the position he had originally adopted, with his head back and his mouth open. He began making the high-pitched whining noise and flicked his long tongue in and out. To my disgust, Beatrice, instead of holding out the meat flat in the palm of her hand as I had done, was able to lean over him and drop it into his mouth. The chick hardly chewed it before gulping it down, ready for more.

The dragon chick had a voracious appetite. It took Beatrice about half an hour to feed him, but finally the stockpot was empty. The chick, however, continued to hold his head back and his jaws open until I picked up the stockpot in both hands and held it out to him so that he could see that it was empty. The chick looked at me and narrowed his eyes, almost as though he thought that I had somehow hidden the contents. Then he hiccupped three times, stretched and climbed down from his nest, rubbing his scales along Beatrice's legs before climbing back up again. He arranged himself by turning around and around as he had done before, looked at Beatrice one last time, curled his tail in front of him and then put his head down and went to sleep.

Putting a finger to his lips, Dr. Drake pointed towards the door. The time had come to leave. We tiptoed out of the coal shed and Dr. Drake shut the door quietly behind us.

"Don't worry, Daniel," he began. "I am proud of you both—"

But just then, his hand moved towards his waistcoat pocket and I noticed that the gold chain that held his watch was missing.

"Good heavens!" he exclaimed, grinning. "The little blighter's stolen my watch. Dragons don't get past *me* very often."

And he returned into the coal shed with a chuckle.

✳

Having eaten his first meal, the dragon chick slept soundly for the next four days. Each time we went to check up on him, I could see that he had not even changed his position. The weather had become slightly less damp, but there were still occasional downpours, so our indoor lessons continued. Mademoiselle Gamay began the promised lesson about gargouilles. She told us that we might soon have the opportunity to meet one that she knew from Paris. I did my best to pay attention as she described how gargouilles closely resemble the gargoyles found on the sides of old cathedrals. They are experts at keeping still for hours, so as to be unobserved, and are unusual among dragons in that each group of gargouilles inhabiting a particular city forms an extended family group or clan. Elder gargouilles watch over the young firebrands and, especially in cities, are careful to avoid contact with humans — except for a few specially selected dragonologists ('garglers', or *gargouillers*, as they are known in French).

During this time we did not often see Dr. Drake. Now that the dragon chick was safely hatched and entrusted to our care, he spent his time either up in London at Dr. Drake's Dragonalia, which was the headquarters of the S.A.S.D., or in his study. I knew that he had sent Emery to make some enquiries about the whereabouts of our parents and about how the Maharawal was getting on, and I knew that he was waiting for a reply. Whenever we did see him, though, he often looked troubled.

On the morning of the fourth day after the chick had hatched, Beatrice and I were reading about some of the famous buildings that Mademoiselle Gamay had told us were inhabited by gargouilles. Suddenly, we heard a high-pitched whining coming from the coal shed.

"At last!" Beatrice cried. "He has woken up!"

"And he sounds hungry!" I added.

We sprang into action. We ran to the pantry, where a second stockpot full of scraps had been saved along with a pile of old newspapers. We carried them both out to the coal shed.

"I hope he'll let *me* feed him this time," I said.

"Just do what I did," said Beatrice. "I'm sure you'll be fine. You can try first."

We opened the door, and the dragon chick very nearly bowled Beatrice over as he half flew, half jumped up at her and licked her face. Beatrice laughed.

"All right!" she said. "That's enough, now. Get down!"

I laughed as well. And after licking Beatrice's face a

few more times, the chick trotted back to his nest. He made no move to greet — or even look at — me. As he jumped down, I saw that one or two pieces of shiny glass had stuck in his underbelly. And when he reached his nest, I noticed that he had picked the glass and gems out of both the necklace and pewter cup with his claws. He had also grown about a third bigger.

Beatrice wrinkled up her nose.

"What a stench!" she said. The repugnant smell was coming from a pile of dragon dung in the corner. It was plain that the coal shed was going to need cleaning out. It would be some time before our charge was properly lair-trained, so we put papers down around the chick's nest to soak up any mess. Beatrice picked up a spade that Dr. Drake had provided for the purpose and began scooping up the chick's dung and taking it outside.

Meanwhile, I placed some food in the palm of my hand and held it out to the chick warily. But this time he didn't even bother to roar at me. Instead, he flapped his leathery wings, flicked his arrowhead tail, and concentrated his gaze on Beatrice as she went back and forth with the spade. When she didn't pay him any attention, he ran in front of her and rolled over onto his back.

"Well, bother you!" I said.

At that, the chick actually turned his head and stuck out his forked tongue at me!

"It looks as though I will have to feed him again," said Beatrice.

"Yes, I'm sure you'll do a much better job," I said grumpily.

She left the spade outside and took a piece of meat from the stockpot. The chick immediately stretched his head back so that she could drop the pieces into his mouth. When he had finished, he hiccupped again, three times, but did not immediately go to sleep. Instead, he sniffed around his nest and picked up the steel chain in his jaws. He carried it over to Beatrice, shook it and then hid it under some bricks at the edge of his nest. Then he ran up to Beatrice and put his head on one side.

"Oh," said Beatrice with a laugh. "You want me to find it, eh, boy?"

After making a pretence of not being able to, Beatrice found the chain, making a great exclamation of mock surprise as she did so, at which the chick began a sort of snaky dance, wiggling from side to side. Then he came up to Beatrice, playfully tugged the chain from her grasp and hid it again.

"Let me find it this time," I said.

"All right," said Beatrice.

But as soon as I went to where the chick had hidden the chain, he stepped in front of me and stood over it, spreading his wings as wide as they would go and growling for all he was worth.

"Come on," I said. "I only want to play."

I stepped closer to him. The chick arched his back and bared his fangs.

"Daniel, be careful," said Beatrice. "You're frightening him."

Something inside me snapped.

"I can't do anything right, can I?" I shouted. "Why don't you just look after him yourself? After all, that's what you wanted, wasn't it?"

I left the coal shed and ran back into the house, where I went upstairs and entered the boys' dormitory in a very black mood. I flopped down on my bed and stared at the ceiling. I wanted to be alone, so I wasn't happy when Darcy came in about a quarter of an hour later.

"No luck with the dragon chick?" he said.

I shook my head.

Darcy thought for a moment.

"I'll tell you what," he said. "You haven't been to see Jamal for a while. Now that it has stopped raining, why not help me teach him to fly? I'm sure Mademoiselle Gamay won't mind."

"All right," I mumbled. I dragged myself off the bed and followed Darcy downstairs.

We left Castle Drake and headed out into St. Leonard's Forest and along the forest path that led to Jamal's compound. It was very muddy, particularly in a stretch near the house where the footpath joined a bridle path, and we had to concentrate hard as we walked along the edge of it, so as not to get stuck.

When we were past the muddiest bit, Darcy turned to me.

"Don't worry about it too much, Daniel," he said. "The chick will get used to you sooner or later." He paused. "They really hate baths," he added. "But you don't get thanks for every good thing you do."

"But it's not fair!" I said. "I didn't know the chick would hate me. And I can't seem to get anything right in class, either," I added.

"I'm afraid I don't have an elder sister, but it must be annoying, the way Beatrice is so perfect at everything," said Darcy with a laugh.

"Thanks for rubbing it in."

"I was joking. Look, Daniel, you are brilliant with

dragons for someone who's only just started learning about them."

"I'm not as good as Beatrice, though, am I?" I said.

Darcy didn't reply.

Thanks a lot, I thought.

We walked on in silence. We were approaching Jamal's compound.

"*You're* brilliant with dragons, Darcy. Do you think you will ever be Dragon Master?" I asked.

"So that's what this is all about, is it?" said Darcy. "You're upset because you think you won't ever be Dragon Master."

"No," I replied. "I'm upset because Beatrice is such a know-it-all about the dragon chick," I said. "But do you?"

"Think I'll be Dragon Master?" Darcy said. "I don't want to be."

"Why on earth not?" I asked.

"Too much of a headache," he replied. "I like *working* with dragons, not worrying about them. And anyway" — he laughed again — "I can see I'd be up against some stiff competition."

"Maybe I would like to be Dragon Master one day," I said a bit sheepishly. "I wouldn't be that horrible a choice, would I?"

"Well, you're certainly the right age," said Darcy.

"What age is that?" I asked.

Darcy smiled. "The Dragon Master begins to train his or her successor in earnest when the apprentice is about eleven or twelve. Of course, Dragon Masters often train two at a time."

"Is that what happened with Ignatius Crook and Dr. Drake?" I said.

"Yes," he replied. "They went through their apprenticeship together."

"But surely the one who loses out doesn't need to become like Ignatius?"

"Of course not," said Darcy. "Ignatius Crook was just a very bad loser, very bad indeed."

As we reached Jamal's compound, I thought about what Darcy had said about the Dragon Master training two successors. Could Dr. Drake really be training Beatrice and me? Most likely he was training Billy and Alicia, Lord Chiddingfold's children, who had been at Castle Drake earlier in the summer, or Darcy and Beatrice, and not me at all. After all, I was proving to be so rotten at dragonology, I stank.

"I keep the kite here," said Darcy, interrupting my thoughts as he fetched an oilskin bag out of a clump of nearby bushes.

"The kite?"

"For teaching Jamal to fly. You'll see!" he said.

Darcy whistled. In a few moments, the young wyvern came thundering up to the gate and whacked it with his long tail.

"Praisich boyar, Jamal!" shouted Darcy. *"Algrai yaryar* Daniel!"

There was a pause. Jamal's brow wrinkled, as though he were trying to remember something. Then he beat his wings and stamped.

"Prrrraisich hoyarrrri," he said. *"Shumul algrrrri."*

"I didn't know Jamal could speak much Dragonish!" I said.

Darcy beamed at Jamal. *"Shumul algri!"* he said, clapping. He looked at me.

"Oh, Mademoiselle Gamay has been teaching him bits and bobs to help him when he flies home to Africa. *Shumul* is 'Jamal' in Dragonish, by the way. And 'Africa' is..."

"Ufrrrrukh," said Jamal. *"Shumul algrrrri yaryar Ufrrrrukh."*

We both laughed as Darcy unlatched the gate.

✳

Darcy led me to a large clearing in the forest, and Jamal loped after us. Then Darcy unfurled the kite, which was itself fashioned in the shape of a dragon. It had obviously seen a lot of use: it was covered in numerous rips and tears and had been mended with wire several times. It was red and looked like a Chinese *lung*, and its tail had several shiny beads attached to it. As soon as he saw the kite, Jamal started to hop up and down on the tips of his claws, moving his head from side to side like a boxer, as he shifted his weight from one foot to the other. He watched as Darcy showed me how to get the kite up into the sky and manoeuvre it in the wind, letting the string in and out to make it go higher or lower and pulling it back in a series of short jerks whenever it needed more lift. Darcy turned towards Jamal.

"Ready, Jamal?" he asked. "Then let's go!"

"Algrrrroo yaryar Ufrrrrukh!" said Jamal.

"Yes!" Darcy cried. "You *will* fly to Africa. But first you've got to fly up to those trees."

Darcy handed the kite to me and shouted to Jamal, *"Gerupthar! Gerupthar! Algrai! Algrai!"*

Jamal came running across the clearing, flapping his wings.

"*Shumul algrrrri!*" he answered back.

Then he leaped upwards, flapping his wings some more. He lifted himself ten or fifteen feet off the ground before flapping his way back down again.

"Get the kite up higher!" said Darcy.

"Righto!" I said.

I was getting the hang of flying the kite now. As I ran back and forth over the clearing, it swerved across the sky, the shiny baubles on its tail flashing. This caught Jamal's attention, and he tried again, loping across the grass underneath the kite and then bending his scaly knees, ready for another leap.

"*Gerupthar! Algrai!*" shouted Darcy. "*Gerupthar!*"

Jamal leaped upwards again, his eyes fixed on the kite's shiny tail. He beat his wings and rose ten, fifteen, twenty, twenty-five feet until he was nearly touching the tail. Then he lunged at it, lost his rhythm and glided back down to the ground.

I had an idea. I reined in the kite a little.

"Let's try again," I said.

"All right," said Darcy.

Jamal was getting bored with the game. This time I had to fly the kite low, running right in front of his face, in order to get him interested.

"Get the kite up higher!" said Darcy.

"Gerupthar! Algrai!" I shouted.

"Gerupthar!" yelled Darcy.

Jamal lurched forwards, trying to get hold of the tail once more, but I pulled the kite up a bit higher. He backed away and took three steps, then launched himself upwards, waving his wings almost as if he were treading water. He started to rise, ten, twenty, twenty-five feet. As he got near the kite, I let the string out and ran backwards, pulling hard to give the kite more lift. Jamal carried on following the tail — he was now thirty feet off the ground. He had nearly reached it, but before he could snap at the baubles, I changed course and pulled it to the left. Jamal followed. I pulled the kite under him and to the right. He dropped after it, so I tugged it over to the left. Again, he followed.

"He's getting it!" exclaimed Darcy. "He's really getting it!"

I let the kite out on its string as far as it would go and ran back across the clearing once more. There was no doubt about it. This was no extended leap. Jamal was flying properly! His instincts had finally kicked in! I pulled the kite down a little, but as I tugged it to the right again, he anticipated me and, with two quick movements, caught it in his teeth and tore it in two, so that the tattered fragments fell out of the sky and landed in a tree. Jamal, however, didn't glide down after them. He stayed in the air, flapping his wings with a gleam in his eye as he circled above us.

"You can do it, Jamal! You can do it!" shouted Darcy. "Good dragon!"

"What now?" I asked.

"I don't think he'll stay up there for long," said Darcy. *"Keramabak!"*

"What does that mean?" I asked.

"It means 'come back'," said Darcy. "But he's never heard that one before."

Instead of coming back, Jamal looked around, as though wondering what to do with his new-found power. He spotted something in the woods and, with a few quick beats of his wings, he was gone.

"How will we get him back?" I shouted.

I needn't have worried. Ten seconds later we heard a loud crash not far away. Jamal might have learned how to fly, but he hadn't learned how to land. He came padding back to the glade with his tail up, looking very pleased with himself.

"Shumul algrrrri yaryar Ufrrrrukh," he said.

✳

I looked up to see a dragon's head grinning down at me...

When the flying lesson was over, Darcy and I furled the kite, put Jamal back in his compound and made our way home through the forest. We had very nearly arrived at Castle Drake when I heard a flapping noise above us and a crashing sound in the trees.

"Oh, no," said Darcy.

"What?" I said.

"It couldn't be—"

"It could," I said.

"Jamal!" he shouted. "Jamal!"

But it wasn't Jamal. Above us, in the branches of a sprawling oak tree, I looked up to see a dragon's head grinning down at me like the Cheshire Cat in *Alice in Wonderland.* It had thick, leathery skin that was greenish-grey, like the lichen that grows on old stones; big, round eyes; long claws; and a thin arrowhead tail that it flicked back and forth. It had perched on a thick branch and didn't look as though it was about to attack, but it could have got to us in a single leap had it chosen to.

"It's a gargouille!" exclaimed Darcy in wonderment.

"Do you know it?" I whispered back.

"No," he replied. "I've never seen a live one before."

I cleared my throat and did my best to sound confident.

"Er, *praisich boyar?*" I said.

"*Prrrraisich hoyarrrri!*" said the dragon. "*Varrrrshch* Drake?*"

"It wants to know if this is the home of Dr. Ernest Drake," Darcy said to me. Then he turned to the dragon and said, "Varshch Drake."

The gargouille scratched his chin with a long, thin claw, grabbed the branch and swung down from the tree so that he was standing right in front of us. He grinned again and bowed.

"*Je m'appelle Panthéon,*" he said.

Now he was talking in French. I tried to remember some.

"Er, *je m'appelle* Daniel," I said. "*Comment... er, comment allez...*"

"*Comment allez vous?*" said Panthéon. "How are you? You do not speak French?"

"Not very well," I admitted.

"Then English must do. You boys are students of Dr. Drake."

"How did you know?" I asked.

"I see children teaching a wyvern to fly in St. Leonard's Forest. I hear one speaking Dragonish well; the other, only a little," said Panthéon. "There can be only one conclusion. But I have urgent news. I must speak to Dr. Drake immediately."

"Dr. Drake isn't here," I said.

"Then I must speak to Mademoiselle Gamay," he said. "Dr. Drake asked me to keep a lookout for two people in my home city, Paris: a man named Ignatius Crook and a Russian woman named Alexandra Gorynytchka. The man I have seen. The woman I have not."

"So Dr. Drake's guess was right," I said with a gasp. "Ignatius really *is* still alive."

Panthéon followed Darcy and me up the gravel drive and waited while Darcy went into the house to fetch Mademoiselle Gamay. She came out with an anxious look on her face. Beatrice came with her.

"Ignatius is still alive," I whispered to my sister.

Her eyes widened.

Panthéon bowed deeply to both of them.

"Is Bernard all right?" asked Mademoiselle Gamay.

"Your brother is well. He sends his greetings," he said. "But as for the rest, it is not good at all. Ignatius Crook was in Paris four days ago. He was searching for Miss Gorynytchka. He did not find her. He found me. I encouraged him to leave. Miss Gorynytchka is not in

Paris at present."

"I wouldn't think she would dare return," said Mademoiselle Gamay, "after the trouble she caused last time."

"She has obtained a great deal of power that she did not have before," said Panthéon, "and many new friends. As you know, things have not been easy for gargouilles in Paris. The city is too big; there is too much smoke and too much noise. Our eyes sting and our ears ring. Many young gargouilles are restless. Since Alexandra Gorynytchka was in Paris, they no longer listen to their elders. They are not respectful. She put ideas into their heads. She made them promises, but her promises are all lies."

"What did she promise them?" I asked.

"She promised to give them Paris," said Panthéon. "As though it was theirs in the first place. She told them the day would come when she would let them drive all the humans out."

"Perhaps we should not talk like this in front of these children," said Mademoiselle Gamay.

"I do not agree!" said Panthéon. "They are students of dragonology. It is better that they know the truth — that if Alexandra Gorynytchka has her way, all the remaining dragons in the world will fall under her sway. There will be no wild dragons left to study. There will be no dragonology."

"Why is she doing this?" I asked.

"Because she hates wild dragons. Those she cannot tame or control, she seeks to kill. Believe me. We gargouilles are an ancient race. We know much, we have seen many things and we fear little. But I have seen what Alexandra Gorynytchka is capable of, and I, Panthéon, chief of the gargouilles of Paris — even I am afraid."

Chapter III
Nia Hayes

Children and fire of any kind should be kept as far apart as possible.
— Liber Draconis, 'Bringing Up Humans'

As soon as Panthéon had delivered his message, he took his leave of us with a bow and, running three or four steps and beating his wings, launched himself up into the air to return home. Mademoiselle Gamay set off for the local town so that she could send a telegram to Dr. Drake in London, while Beatrice and I went to look in at the coal shed window, where we saw the dragon chick fast asleep. I told her about teaching Jamal to fly and about how Darcy and I had met Panthéon.

"Alexandra Gorynytchka seems a much, much greater threat than we thought," said Beatrice.

"Yes," I replied. "I thought that she was just interested in stealing back the treasures of the S.A.S.D., but there's obviously more to it than that. Panthéon really seemed to be frightened of her."

"I wonder what happened in Paris," said Beatrice, "with the other gargouilles."

"Perhaps we could ask Dr. Drake," I said.

But when Dr. Drake returned from London later that evening, he went straight into his study with Mademoiselle Gamay, and they stayed there the whole evening. By the time we woke up the next morning, he had already left.

When we asked her, Mademoiselle Gamay would not explain what they had talked about, saying that Panthéon had obviously worried us enough. It was not until a few days later that we found out anything at all.

It was a Saturday morning, and we had not even realised that Dr. Drake had returned from London, when a coach arrived at Castle Drake and out stepped Lord Chiddingfold, the Minister for Dragons; Mr. Tibbs, the Minister's Secretary; and a girl of about Beatrice's age. She had dark skin and two plaits underneath her wide straw hat. She wore a blue knee-length dress and heavy boots. I'd never seen her before, and I wondered who she could be.

"Welcome," said Dr. Drake, stepping out of the house and onto the gravel drive. "Minister. Mr. Tibbs..."

Lord Chiddingfold was tight-lipped as he shook Dr. Drake's hand. Mr. Tibbs was frowning.

"No news from Jaisalmer, I suppose?" he said.

"None so far," said Dr. Drake. "And Panthéon has not returned, either." He turned to the strange girl.

"Nia!" he said, holding out his hand. "I am so glad that you could join us here at Castle Drake. I can see that your journey from Texas has left you none the worse for wear. Daniel, Beatrice," he said, turning to us, "come and meet Nia Hayes from America. Her father, Noah, has gone to Jaisalmer to take over from your parents. She's come to stay with us while he's away."

Beatrice and I came forward and shook the girl's hand. Her grip was pretty strong, and she pumped my hand up and down several times as she said, "It's mighty nice to meet you both. I've never met any other kids who study dragons before."

"So you study dragons too?" asked Beatrice.

"Of course!" said Nia. "As far back as I can remember. My daddy runs a sort of dragon orphanage out at a ranch called Elmo's Creek near El Paso, Texas. I've raised five moth dragons from the egg."

"Well, Beatrice and I are raising a baby European dragon at the moment," I said. "Or, at least, Beatrice is," I added. "He won't let me near him because I had to dunk him in a bucket of water to cool him down."

"Oh, I wouldn't let him get away with that," said Nia with a smile. "My daddy says you've got to show dragon chicks tough love sometimes. They get over it. The Minister told me about your chick on the way down here," said Nia. "Does he have a name yet?"

"Not yet. Dr. Drake says that we should choose a name based on something he does, and he hasn't done very much yet, apart from eat, sleep and steal Dr. Drake's pocket watch," said Beatrice.

"Indeed," said Dr. Drake. "I think the little fellow is sleeping right now, so if you are quiet, you might all be able to take a look at him — if his guardians don't mind, of course." He gave Beatrice and me a wink and a broad smile.

"We'd be delighted!" exclaimed Beatrice. "Come with us and we'll show you." She linked arms with Nia and began to lead her towards the coal shed.

"I say, Drake," cut in Lord Chiddingfold, before Beatrice and Nia had got very far. "I don't want to be rude, but Tibbs and I didn't come all the way down from London to go goo-ing and gah-ing over a newly hatched dragon chick. We've got some business to discuss, and we'd like to get on with it, if we may. Shall we go into your study, perhaps?"

If Dr. Drake was taken aback by Lord Chiddingfold's tone, he didn't show it. Instead, he simply looked at him and replied, "Of course, Minister, you are right. Children, perhaps you could entertain our American guest by introducing her to the dragon chick. Gentlemen, if you would please come with me?" He set off, and Lord Chiddingfold and Mr. Tibbs followed him into the house.

Beatrice turned to Nia and said, "Don't mind Lord Chiddingfold. He's always grumpy with Dr. Drake about something."

"He's grumpy, for sure," said Nia. "But it's the other one who's really sour. The whole way here from London he had his lips pursed so hard I thought he must have eaten a whole basket of lemons!"

Beatrice laughed. "Well, come and meet our dragon chick. He's been known to be a bit grumpy as well, but only with Daniel so far."

They linked arms again, and walked together towards the coal shed. I followed behind. It seemed as though they were becoming fast friends already. *Just as long as Beatrice doesn't let Nia feed the chick before me,* I thought. It was *our* dragon chick, after all.

Beatrice pushed open the shed door and led the way

inside. The chick was sound asleep on top of his nest, his legs splayed out and his snout resting next to the steel chain, as though he had fallen asleep playing with it.

"Oh, my goodness! He's mighty sweet, isn't he?" exclaimed Nia — a little too loudly, I thought.

The chick gave a shudder, and his eyes blinked open. When he saw Nia, he instinctively put out his foreleg and clutched his favourite treasures to himself. Then he looked at Beatrice, gave a happy wriggle and stretched out his tail. Beatrice went over to him, and he let her pick him up in her arms and show him to Nia. As Nia bent to look at him, he put out his forked tongue.

"Excuse me, buster," said Nia, wagging a stern finger at him. "But that's no way to treat a lady." She laughed at the puzzled expression on the chick's face, then reached out her hand and gently stroked the scales along his back. To my horror, the chick seemed to like it and curled his back upwards into a bow shape as his head and tail quivered.

"My, but he's soft, isn't he?" she said. "He's even softer than a baby amphithere's tail feathers."

"Dr. Drake says his scales will take a few weeks to harden," said Beatrice. "But he's growing so rapidly that he'll probably shed his first lot of skin within a few days."

"Of course, it won't be as flameproof as it will be when he's older," I added. "But Dr. Drake says it will still be worth keeping. I thought I might use it to make a pair of flameproof gloves for my next field expedition."

"Your *next* field expedition?" said Beatrice. "Daniel, you haven't even gone on your first yet."

I ignored her.

"Gloves would be a fine idea, Daniel," said Nia. "For my birthday last year, my daddy gave me a pair of flameproof gloves made from the shed skin off the big Mex that lives up on the hill behind our ranch. I brought them with me. I can show you later."

I just nodded. Nia certainly seemed to know a lot about dragons. I just hoped that she wouldn't turn out to be as much of a show-off about it as Beatrice could sometimes be.

"Does the chick often get hungry?" asked Nia.

"He gets very hungry," said Beatrice. "But he only needs to eat every four or five days. He likes to play, too, although he's a bit sleepy at the moment."

"All chicks like to play!" said Nia. "It doesn't sound as if European dragons are that much different from moth dragons. I can see you've got a way with dragon chicks, Beatrice. My daddy says that some people are just plain born to work with dragons, while others will never have the slightest clue."

She looked at me. My expression must have given away my feelings, because she said, "Gosh, Daniel, I didn't mean you." Then she thought for a moment and added, "Do you know? One way you can get a chick to like you is by showing it something it really wants. Something bright and shiny, like a rhinestone bracelet or some pieces of coloured glass. Why don't you try that?"

"Well, I was already planning to do something like that," I said.

Beatrice opened her mouth to speak, but just then the chick, which she was still holding, let out an enormous yawn.

"Aww," said Nia. "He's just as drowsy as a bear cub in winter."

"We should let him go back to sleep," said Beatrice.

She put the chick down on the top of his nest and turned to leave.

"I think I'll come out in a minute," I said.

"Why's that?" said Beatrice.

Without letting the chick see, I showed them a coin I had taken from my pocket.

"I might try this," I said.

"Well, I'd polish it first, Daniel, but good luck!" said Beatrice. "Don't be too long. And don't frighten him again."

And with that, she left the coal shed with Nia following her.

When the chick and I were alone, I put the coin back in my pocket. He was pretending to be asleep, but I could tell that he was secretly watching my every move, in case I decided to try to steal some of his treasure.

I knew I shouldn't do it, but instead of the coin, I took the pieces of flint and iron pyrites that I always carried around with me out of my pocket.

"Look," I whispered, holding the stones out to him.

The dragon looked at the stones and tilted his head to one side.

"One day you'll be able to do this!" I said, even though I knew he couldn't understand me. I struck the stones together and made a bright shower of sparks.

The chick stood up. His eyes flashed with interest. I did it again.

He padded towards me.

At last! I thought.

I held the stones just out of reach. The chick began to trot and then to run around me, jumping playfully as he tried to grab the stones from my hand. He beat his wings furiously, but he was too young to fly.

"No," I said with a laugh, holding the stones above my head. "Not for you." The chick leaped up again and again, but he couldn't reach them.

"These are mine," I said. "You're too small to make fire yet. You'll have to find your own when you get a bit bigger. But at least you know what to look for now."

I put the stones back in my pocket. The dragon chick's eyes had never left them for a moment, but once they were gone, he retreated to the top of his nest, looking at my pocket out of the corner of his eye.

"I'll be back next time you want a feed," I said to him. "And then we'll see who you like best, eh?"

I knew I was being silly, but I didn't care. I went to

the door. But before I opened it, the chick came down off the top of his nest and rubbed his scales across my legs, exactly as he had done with Beatrice. He actually liked me at last!

Outside, Beatrice and Nia were waiting for me.

"Well?" said Nia.

"I think it worked," I said.

"Really?" said Beatrice. She sounded sceptical. "You're sure that you didn't upset him?"

She had a real way of needling me when she wanted to.

"Of course not," I retorted loudly.

"You *are* touchy today, Daniel," said Beatrice. She turned to Nia. "Now, Nia, have you ever met a knucker? We've got one here in the forest. Her name's Weasel, and she's not the cleverest of dragons, but she's ever so easy to track. Would you like to meet her?"

Nia nodded.

"I'd like that very much," said Nia. "Thank you. And on the way, I'll tell you about the time I went to Canada to look for frost dragons."

We began to walk up the path towards the forest. Suddenly, there was a commotion from inside the coal shed. It sounded as though the chick was banging and thumping on the door. We ran back to the shed, but before we got there, the noise subsided.

We looked in at the window. The chick was curled up on top of his nest as though nothing had happened.

"Are you quite sure you didn't frighten him, Daniel?" said Beatrice suspiciously.

"Of course not," I said. Then from inside the shed came the sound of a loud hiccup.

"You're quite sure you didn't feed him anything?" said Beatrice.

"Like what?" I said.

"If I find out that you've done anything stupid, I will be very, very cross," said Beatrice.

"I've already told you I didn't, haven't I?" I shouted. "But you obviously don't believe me, so why should I tell you again? Well, don't let me get in the way of you introducing Nia to Weasel. I suppose I'd better not come, just in case I 'do anything stupid'. You'll be much better off without me!"

And I stormed back to the house.

*I crept to the side of the house and crouched down underneath
Dr. Drake's study window…*

Chapter IV
DESPERATE DANGER

The rare but disturbing fashion for dragon keeping must be discouraged with fire and claw wherever it is found.
— Liber Draconis, 'Humanology: Notes on Our Unscaly Friends'

I had got as far as the drive in front of Castle Drake when my angry thoughts were interrupted by raised voices coming from Dr. Drake's study. Lord Chiddingfold, Mr. Tibbs and Dr. Drake were engaged in a heated discussion. Although I knew that it was wrong, I crept to the side of the house and crouched down underneath Dr. Drake's study window in order to hear what they were saying.

"...the fact is," said Mr. Tibbs, "as British Dragon Master, it is your job to stay here to conserve and protect *British* dragons, not to go gallivanting around the world as a... as a... universal dragon saviour!"

"Quite," said Lord Chiddingfold. "I'm sure Monsieur

Gamay and the French Dragon Master can deal with a few uppity gargouilles. Meanwhile, let the Maharawal resolve the problems in Jaisalmer. We have already sent help twice. You yourself admit that the disease that is affecting the nagas has not, so far, proved life threatening."

"But don't you see that these problems are linked?" said Dr. Drake. "Although we sent the Cooks to Jaisalmer, they have not been able to get to the bottom of the naga situation, and now it's getting worse. And thanks to Ignatius Crook, we know that Alexandra Gorynytchka has been conducting some sort of heinous experiments, which apparently 'achieved some remarkable results' among the nagas of northern India. And it's Gorynytchka who also appears to have caused the upset in Paris. We simply *must* find out what she is up to."

"They are hardly remarkable results if the illness has been at large for so long and not a single naga has died from it," said Lord Chiddingfold.

"Honestly, Drake," said Mr. Tibbs. "Do you really expect us to believe *everything* Ignatius Crook says? It's far more likely that this Russian woman is nothing more than a thief who will be brought to justice in due course."

"Yes, she is a thief," retorted Dr. Drake. "But you

underestimate her at your peril! You have read Bernard Gamay's report, have you not? It makes chilling reading. When Miss Gorynytchka applied to join the French Dragonological Society, he investigated her background. She was born in Siberia to an aristocratic family of dragon keepers, but there was a terrible episode that resulted in a small army of wild dragons slaying her entire family when she was young. She has hated wild dragons ever since. Now, in revenge, she seeks to tame all dragons and bend them to her will."

"'And those dragons that she cannot conquer, she desires to kill,'" interrupted Mr. Tibbs. "Yes, we have read Monsieur Gamay's report, thank you. But it is still not *proof* that Miss Gorynytchka is behind the disturbances among the gargouilles, nor that she has anything to do with naga sickness. And it is proof that we need!"

"But what of the other rumours?" said Dr. Drake. "Apart from the outrages committed by some of the younger gargouilles, frost dragons have been spotted out of season flying south instead of north, and a mass of black European dragons have been seen flying eastwards during broad daylight. Something is terribly amiss. There is even a rumour that the same disease that is affecting the nagas has now spread to the Chinese *lung*. I have asked Panthéon to investigate that rumour himself via the network of intelligent dragons."

"Jolly good, Drake, jolly good. I'm not sure that bringing in a French dragon to investigate the problem is exactly how we at the Ministry of Dragons would have tackled things, but I have no doubt that he will find these rumours to be exactly that — just rumours," said Lord Chiddingfold.

"Let us hope so, Minister," said Mr. Tibbs. "And let us not forget that one of the chief aims of the Secret and Ancient Society of Dragonologists is to keep the existence of dragons a secret! The Prime Minister is also extremely concerned about the potential embarrassment that could be caused by the fact that three of the twelve treasures of the Society have now been stolen. He is worried that the powerful artefacts supposedly safely in the care of British dragons may soon become implicated in a number of dragon disasters abroad. The recovery of those treasures from Miss Gorynytchka must be our prime task, and one that we believe should be entrusted to Emery Cloth."

"Indeed," said Lord Chiddingfold. "Unless this becomes a bona fide global emergency, Drake, then I cannot and will not give my permission for you to leave your post here. Besides, it is essential that you prepare that wyvern, Jamal, for his imminent return to Africa. His constant escapes are a worry we can do without."

"Minister," said Dr. Drake, "I must ask you to think again. Noah Hayes—"

But before Dr. Drake could say any more, a sudden explosion drowned out his voice and seemed to rock the house to its very foundations. I jumped.

"What on earth...?" cried Dr. Drake.

The noise had come from the other side of the house, and as I ran towards it, I had a terrible premonition. I felt in my pockets. The pieces of flint and iron pyrites had gone. The chick must have stolen them when he was rubbing against my legs. How could I have been so stupid?

I raced around the side of Castle Drake to find the coal shed ablaze. Flames curled round the edge of the roof, and smoke poured out from under the door. I could hear agitated noises coming from within and the sound of desperate, repeated butting against the door. The dragon chick was trapped inside!

"Help!" I cried. "The coal shed is going up like a torch!"

Dr. Drake rushed out of the house and ran to the shed. He grabbed the door handle but immediately let go — it was already too hot to touch. Beatrice, Nia, and Darcy came running across the lawn from the direction of the forest.

"The dragon chick!" cried Beatrice. "We've got to get the dragon chick out at once!"

"Out of the way! *Vite!*" cried Mademoiselle Gamay as she barged past us with a pan full of water, which she flung onto the flames.

"Right," called Dr. Drake, taking the lead. "We must use water from the pond to put out the fire. Beatrice and Darcy, fetch buckets, pans, anything you can find to carry it. Daniel, run to my study and get my flameproof cloak and gloves. You'll find them with the rest of the field equipment in a large chest by the window. Everyone else, form a human chain from the pond."

I rushed into the house. When I returned, I saw that Beatrice and Darcy had already collected several containers and given them to Mademoiselle Gamay, who was scooping water out of the pond and passing the containers to Lord Chiddingfold, who passed them to Mr. Tibbs, who passed them to Nia Hayes. Nia took them and energetically emptied them over the burning shed, then passed them back.

"Hand me the flameproof cloak, and put on those gloves, Daniel," said Dr. Drake.

I pulled on the gloves while Dr. Drake flung his cap to the floor and opened the flameproof cloak in front of him.

"Right, Nia," he said, crouching down in front of the shed. "When Daniel opens the door, throw your next bucket of water inside. I am going to try to catch the dragon chick when he comes out. He will be hot, so if I miss him, whatever you do, don't let him touch you."

I stood as close to the door as I dared.

"Now, Daniel!" cried Dr. Drake. "Be quick!"

I tore open the shed door, and both Beatrice and Nia hurled buckets of water inside. The frightened dragon chick shot through the ring of flames straight towards Dr. Drake. He tried to dodge between Dr. Drake's legs, but in a swift gesture Dr. Drake caught him in the flameproof cloak and wrapped it around him, until he was no more than a wriggling bundle.

"Here," he said, holding the bundle out towards me. "You deal with him."

"What should I do?"

"The pond," said Dr. Drake. "You must cool him down. You'll have to wade in, I'm afraid."

I didn't relish the idea of dunking the chick again, but I took him towards the pond. Lord Chiddingfold and Mr. Tibbs were still passing containers of water to Beatrice and Nia to throw on the flames, while Darcy returned the empty ones to Mademoiselle Gamay to refill.

When I reached the pond, I unravelled the chick from the cloak, taking care to touch him only with the flameproof gloves. As I waded into the pond, he realised what I was going to do and struggled with all his might. He flapped his wings wildly and kicked his legs. I was soon soaked by all the splashing. But, keeping a firm grip on him, I dunked him down beneath the water. Immediately a cloud of steam hissed from the surface, and a trail of bubbles rose from the chick's nostrils as I briefly held him under. Then I let him go, and he splashed out of the pond and stood in front of Dr. Drake, shaking droplets off his scales like a wet dog.

I squelched my way out of the pond and joined Dr. Drake in front of the coal shed. The blaze was finally out, but the inside of the shed was a mess. The walls were charred and black with soot. Most of the coal had burned, and the rest was still glowing. Luckily the chick's nest was mostly metal and had resisted the flames.

"Poor little thing!" said Beatrice, panting as she recovered from the effort of hauling so many buckets of water. She looked at the bedraggled dragon chick. "How on earth can it have happened?"

At that very moment, the dragon shook his head and hiccupped. Then he opened his jaws and blew out a long, thin stream of blue flame.

"The devil!" exclaimed Lord Chiddingfold. "He can breathe fire already! How on earth...?"

Dr. Drake looked in my direction and cleared his throat.

Everyone's eyes were upon me.

"I think that the chick must have stolen the pieces of flint and iron pyrites I carry in my pocket," I said in a small voice.

"Stolen them?" said Beatrice "But how did he know that you had them?"

"Well," I said, my ears burning, "I might have shown them to him and struck them together to show him how to make sparks."

"Against my orders," said Dr. Drake sternly. "And against all dragonological common sense!"

Beatrice looked at me enquiringly, but I looked down at the ground, feeling decidedly sheepish.

"You actually showed him how to make sparks with them?" exclaimed Darcy.

"And he stole them from you?" said Nia. "Without you *even noticing?*"

"I'm speechless, Daniel," said Beatrice.

"I believe you should take extremely stern measures with this boy," said Lord Chiddingfold.

"The sternest possible," agreed Mr. Tibbs.

There was an uncomfortable pause. *This is it,* I thought. *I'm bound to be expelled from the S.A.S.D. this time.*

Then the dragon chick stood up and waddled over towards me. He rubbed his side along the back of my legs and looked up at me.

At least I have one friend, I thought.

"Hey," said Nia, "we can give the chick a name now!"

"What's that?" said Beatrice.

"Don't you remember that Daniel said that the shed was 'going up like a torch'? You told me that this chick's brother is called Scorcher. So why don't we call this little fellow Torcher?"

"Yes," said Beatrice sarcastically. "Why not? I think Torcher will be a very good name, don't you, Daniel? Then we'll always remember how he got it, won't we?"

I thought it was a good name, too, but I didn't say anything. I was still waiting to find out whether I would be expelled or not. Just then, I heard a boy shouting loudly at the front of the house and ringing the doorbell.

"Hello? Hello?" he called. "Is there anyone at home? I've got an urgent telegram for Dr. Drake."

Lord Chiddingfold and Mr. Tibbs exchanged glances.

"I'm afraid I shall have to deal with you later, Daniel," said Dr. Drake, walking towards the house before disappearing around the side.

He soon came back, reading the telegram and shaking his head in disbelief.

"What is it?" Mr. Tibbs asked. "Is it news from Jaisalmer?"

"Yes," said Dr. Drake. He held it out for Lord Chiddingfold and Mr. Tibbs to see. They both looked astonished.

"Does it say if my daddy's arrived in Jaisalmer yet?" said Nia.

"No," said Dr. Drake. "It doesn't say whether he has arrived there or not."

"What about *our* parents?" asked Beatrice.

My throat felt dry.

Dr. Drake passed the telegram to us.
It was from the Maharawal of Jaisalmer. It said:

NAGA ILLNESS FATAL.
DRAGONS IN DESPERATE DANGER.
COOKS VANISHED.
COME QUICKLY.

Chapter V
DRAKE DEPARTS

Honorific-abilitudini-tatibus (Latin): The quality or state of deserving honour; a quality possessed by the noble dragons of the Dragon Express.
— Liber Draconis, 'Glossary'

Surely you will agree that this is a bona fide emergency?" said Dr. Drake to Lord Chiddingfold and Mr. Tibbs. "Two British dragonologists are missing! I must go to India to find them."

"I thought that our parents were on a ship," I said. "You said that they were on their way home."

"As indeed they should be," said Dr. Drake. "They must never have made it on board."

"How are *you* going to get there?" cried Beatrice. "The journey must take at least four weeks, to begin with!"

"Do not worry," said Dr. Drake "The Dragon Express will get me there much faster than that."

"Hold on, Drake," said Mr. Tibbs. "No one has taken the Dragon Express for over one hundred and fifty years."

"Nevertheless, I will take it," said Dr. Drake.

"Drake, I don't like it. I don't like it one bit," said Lord Chiddingfold. "But I know that there's no way of persuading you against it now, and so I won't stand in your way. But for heaven's sake be careful. Mr. Tibbs, I fear that we must return to London at once to inform the Prime Minister of this turn of events. He is not going to be a happy man."

"Thank you, Minister," said Dr. Drake.

And with that, Dr. Drake sent Darcy to ask the carriage driver to take Lord Chiddingfold and Mr. Tibbs back home to London with as much speed as he could manage.

After they had left, Beatrice asked, "Is there anything we can do to help?"

"First," said Dr. Drake, "you and Nia had better take care of Torcher while Daniel gets changed out of those wet clothes and clears up the mess in the coal shed," said Dr. Drake. He turned to me. "You must be extremely careful not to leave anything flammable in there now," he said rather sternly, but then he grinned and gave me a wink before heading into the house.

I breathed a sigh of relief. I was not going to be expelled from the S.A.S.D. after all. Once Dr. Drake had gone, I turned to my sister.

"Bea," I said, "I'm really sorry about what happened with Torcher."

"Oh, don't worry about that any more, Daniel," she said. "The important thing now is to help Dr. Drake find Mother and Father."

"He will find them, won't he?"

"Yes, of course he will," she said. But she didn't sound sure.

I turned and went into the house, kicked off my wet shoes, and ran up to the boys' dormitory, where I changed my damp trousers and socks. I emerged from the house a few minutes later to find Nia and Beatrice chasing after Torcher, who was running between their legs as they tried to grab something he had in his mouth.

"I'm afraid Torcher managed to steal Mr. Tibbs's pocket watch," said Beatrice. "I'm sure he will be furious when he finds out. It's got a lovely picture of a wyvern on it, but it's already been badly dented."

Dr. Drake soon emerged from the house, carrying a stick and a small haversack and pulling his magnificent dragon saddle behind him. He stopped in the centre of his lawn, reached into his waistcoat pocket, and took out what I recognised as a dragon whistle. He blew three short blasts on it. Torcher immediately dropped Mr. Tibbs's pocket watch and ran over to him. A few moments later, both Jamal and Weasel were also poking their heads out of the undergrowth at the edge of St. Leonard's Forest, attracted by the whistle's peculiar sound.

"Sorry, Jamal," said Dr. Drake. "You are not big enough to take me on your back just yet. Dominique, would you mind?"

Mademoiselle Gamay went over to the edge of the forest to lead Jamal away, pausing to shoo Weasel off with a few loud shouts. She turned around just before disappearing into the woods, looking worried.

"*Au revoir*, Ernest," she called. "Please take care."

"Don't worry, my friend," he replied. "I will be back as soon as I can." He turned to us. "Beatrice, Daniel, I'm going to do everything I can to find your parents, but I may be gone for some time. In the meantime, you must remain here to look after young Torcher and help Nia settle in. I fear that Jamal will need to return to Africa very soon. But don't worry; Panthéon is going to help prepare him for his release. He will know what to do if and when the time comes. I shall be in touch with Panthéon via the network of intelligent dragons, and if there is any news, he will bring it to you."

Dr. Drake scanned the skies expectantly. We looked up too.

"Who is Panthéon?" whispered Nia. "I have heard his name before."

"He's a gargouille," I said.

"A French dragon?" said Nia.

"Yes," said Beatrice. "He lives on the roof of the Panthéon, a large church in Paris."

"Might he come if he hears the dragon whistle, do you think?" asked Nia.

"Maybe, but he's too small for Dr. Drake to ride on," said Beatrice.

We continued looking upwards. After a while, a small green dot appeared high overhead. It got bigger and bigger until a huge European dragon swooped down and landed on Dr. Drake's lawn. He was so big that his scaly, horned head was almost level with the tops of the trees. He was called Idraigir; Beatrice and I had met him — and ridden on him — during our last adventure, searching for the fabled gem known as the Dragon's Eye. Idraigir turned towards us and swung his head down low enough so that his dinner-plate-sized eyes were on the same level as ours. Nia gasped. Clearly, she had never seen a full-sized European dragon before. Beatrice picked up Torcher and held him in her arms.

"Greetings," said Idraigir. "Do not worry about the chick, Beatrice. You may put him down."

Beatrice put Torcher on the ground. As soon as he realised he was free, he ran and hid himself behind her legs. Idraigir lowered his head even further, so that his chin rested on the ground and his eyes were almost level with the chick. It was amazing to think that little Torcher would one day grow to such a monstrous size.

"*Prrrraisich boyarrrr,*" said Idraigir to the dragon chick, along with a string of other Dragonish phrases that I had never heard before. I did not think Torcher would be likely to understand the words, but he looked back at Idraigir with round, wondering eyes. Then he emerged from behind Beatrice's legs, padded over to Idraigir, and sniffed him. Idraigir sniffed back and looked up to speak to us.

"A very interesting meeting," he said. "Where is his lair?"

I pointed towards the coal shed.

"I need to rebuild it," I said. "There was an accident."

"Prrrraisich boyarrrr," *said Idraigir to the dragon chick…*

"Not the sort of place I would choose for a lair," said Idraigir, "but it will do for the time being. You had better hold on to him when I go."

Beatrice bent down, picked up Torcher, and held him in her arms.

"I am grateful to you for coming, Idraigir," said Dr. Drake. "I do not have much time. You gave me a ride not so long ago. If you are willing, I would be most thankful for another."

"You will certainly be in my debt then," said Idraigir. "Will we be travelling far? I must not stay away from my lair for long, as you know."

"I need to fly east. To the Harz Mountains, in Germany," said Dr. Drake.

"Then it is to the Harz Mountains that we shall go," said Idraigir.

And so, without more ado, Dr. Drake picked up the dragon saddle and fastened it across Idraigir's back, tightening the long straps underneath the dragon's huge belly. He fastened his haversack to the pommel of the saddle, picked up his stick, and swung himself up onto Idraigir's back.

"Remember," he said to us, "be kind hosts to Nia, and take care of Jamal and Torcher. And Beatrice, don't be hard on Daniel; I am sure that he has learned his lesson. I will contact you as soon as possible, but in the meantime, try not to worry — I'm sure your parents are safe and that there is some logical explanation for all this. Above all, remember your dragonological training at all times, and — be brave!"

Idraigir took off and soared up into the sky. As I watched Dr. Drake rise high into the air, I asked, "How will Dr. Drake get to India if Idraigir is only taking him as far as Germany?"

"He'll use the Dragon Express," said Nia.

"What is the Dragon Express?" asked Beatrice.

"It's a form of travel once used by expert dragonologists," answered Nia. "My daddy told me about it. It's a bit like a stagecoach. Only instead of taking teams of horses, you catch a dragon, who gives you a ride to the next dragon, who lets you ride him to the next, and so on."

"How long will it take?" I asked.

"To get to India? That depends which route Dr. Drake takes," she said. "He might go directly east, which would be quicker, or south, which would be warmer. If he goes east, it might take only a few days. If he goes south, it might take a week or even more."

"But how do you know which dragons are part of the Dragon Express?" I asked.

"There's a special password you have to use," said Nia.

"Do you know what it is?" I asked her.

"No," said Nia. "I don't even know if my daddy knows what it is. He says it is only taught to advanced dragonologists, so the Dragon Express can only be used in real dragon emergencies. There is always a chance, you see, that the dragons will be spotted if they spend too much time away from their home range. To cross mountains, they have to fly low; otherwise, their riders would have trouble breathing. The air gets thinner the higher up you go, you see."

I nodded. I remembered noticing how thin the air was when I had flown back from Scotland on Idraigir with Dr. Drake and Beatrice.

For the next few days, I turned to the task of clearing out the coal shed. First I swept out all the ashes. Most of the shed was made of stone and hadn't burned too badly, but many of the beams were scorched black. Torcher's 'treasures' were undamaged, so I rearranged them on top of the pile of bricks. Nia even came and helped me, while Beatrice looked after Torcher.

Although both Beatrice and I were very worried about our parents, we reassured each other that Dr. Drake would find them, and all would be well. All the same, we spent a lot of our time standing in the garden of Castle Drake, peering up into the sky, both day and night, for any sign of Panthéon. Meanwhile, Darcy and Mademoiselle Gamay continued to look after Jamal, who had started flying further and further afield, and, helped by Nia, who had soon settled into life at Castle Drake, Beatrice and I took care of Torcher. Much to my relief and pleasure, the fast-growing fellow was now happy to let me feed him.

Torcher slept most of the time, but when he was awake, he was becoming a real handful. He was extremely clever at stealing anything shiny that he took a fancy to — which proved to be almost *everything* shiny — and included two buttons from my Sunday jacket, a hatpin from Nia's straw hat, and, on one occasion, one of Mademoiselle Gamay's diamond stud earrings. How she did not notice when he stole it right out of her earlobe I will never know, but it made us keep a very close eye on him. Another time, we were playing with him in the garden when, unbeknown to us, Weasel was hunting rabbits nearby. The knucker came streaking out of the undergrowth, followed by the naughty dragon chick playfully nipping at her heels.

"I hope he doesn't try that with Jamal," said Beatrice.

One morning as I was returning to Castle Drake after helping Darcy with another of Jamal's flying lessons, Beatrice came running towards me.

"Nia and I have made an important dragonological discovery!" she said. "Come quickly!"

"What is it?" I asked.

"You'll see," she said. "Follow me."

She grabbed my arm and led me to the coal shed, where Nia was playing with Torcher.

"Nia," said Beatrice, "show Daniel what we've discovered."

"Oh! You are gonna love this!" said Nia. "See how Torcher likes being tickled on his belly?" And she gave Torcher's stomach a good scratch, which made him wriggle and chirp. "But watch what happens when I tickle him here." And she tickled him under the chin. Torcher sat up, gave a rattly kind of hiccup, then shot out a thin blue jet of flame.

"You made him breathe fire!" I exclaimed.

"Yes!" Beatrice said. "He does it every time."

"Let me try," I said. I reached over and gave Torcher a

The knucker came streaking out of the undergrowth,
followed by the naughty dragon chick...

scratch and a tickle under his chin, and, sure enough, he hiccupped and spat out another flame. We had found a way of getting him to breathe fire on cue!

✳

It was on a day when Torcher was asleep, and Beatrice, Nia, Darcy and I had been to see Jamal, that Panthéon finally visited us again. We found him waiting for us on the lawn of Castle Drake as we returned from the forest. Dr. Drake had several statues of dragons dotted about the grounds of his house and, for a brief moment, I thought that perhaps he had had another delivered. But then Panthéon turned to look in our direction. Now I understood how gargouilles could camouflage themselves simply by not moving.

"Praisich boyar, Panteoo!" I said, using the Dragonish pronunciation of Panthéon's name.

"Prrrraisich hoyarrrri!" called back Panthéon.

"So this is a gargouille?" said Nia. "Mighty pleased to meet you."

She took Panthéon's front claw and did her best to shake it.

"And I to meet you," he said. *"Je suis enchanté,* although I wish it could be in happier circumstances. A terrible evil has entered the world of dragons, and

❧ 94 ❧

I must speak with Mademoiselle Gamay urgently. Is she here?"

Beatrice went into the house to fetch Mademoiselle Gamay, who came out to join us.

"Dr. Drake has arrived in Jaisalmer," said Panthéon.

"Has he found out anything about our parents?" asked Beatrice.

"They are alive. But he believes that they have been kidnapped."

"Kidnapped!" exclaimed Beatrice. "By whom?"

"Dr. Drake's suspicions rest squarely with Alexandra Gorynytchka," said Panthéon. "I am afraid that your parents are not the only dragonologists to have disappeared during the last week or two—"

"But why would Miss Gorynytchka kidnap our parents?" I said.

"We do not yet know," said Panthéon. "There has been no communication with her. But rest assured of one thing: Dr. Drake will find them, wherever they are. He will make sure that they are rescued."

"What about my daddy, Noah?" said Nia. "Is there any news of him?"

"Your father arrived in Jaisalmer some weeks ago. Despite hearing about the suspected kidnappings, he refused to be put off his mission and has bravely travelled into the Thar Desert to try to help any nagas who are still alive. I only hope that he finds some. After years of producing only mild symptoms, the sickness among the nagas has suddenly evolved into a highly infectious disease that now kills dragons within days. More terrible still is that the sickness is now affecting dragons other than nagas. A *lung* that had gone to the aid of the nagas became infected and unwittingly carried the disease back to China. Now, several other *lung* are showing early symptoms. If it keeps spreading like this, who knows where it will end?"

"But there is one thing that I do not understand," I said. "If Alexandra Gorynytchka wants to tame and control dragons, why would she unleash a deadly plague that threatens to destroy them? It just does not make any sense."

"You are right," said Panthéon. "It does not seem logical. But there is bound to be some rational explanation. And you may not know this, but Miss Gorynytchka is not the first dragonologist to have meddled with dragons and achieved results that were both unforeseen and unwanted."

I nodded. I had a feeling that I knew what he meant.

"There is one more thing," added Panthéon.
"Dr. Drake has asked me to contact the British Society
of Dragons to see if they can do anything to help. I will
visit them today, just as soon as I have visited Jamal.
Then I must return to Paris at once, for I fear there is
more trouble brewing among the gargouilles."

And with that, Panthéon took his leave of us and
disappeared into the trees.

That night I could hardly sleep for worrying about
my parents and wondering whether the British Society
of Dragons could possibly help.

The next morning, Beatrice, Nia, Darcy, and I were
on the lawn playing with Torcher when we heard the
doorbell ring. Hoping that it might be a letter or news
from Dr. Drake, I rushed round to the front of the
house with the others to find Mademoiselle Gamay
bending down to examine a slim piece of grey, sloughed-
off dragon hide. There was no sign of whoever or
whatever had left it there, but when I leaned over to
look at it myself, I saw at once that it was covered in
dragon runes. Beatrice and I had studied the rune
alphabet with Dr. Drake, and we were able to translate it
quickly; this was fortunate, for the writing on the grey

hide began to vanish almost as quickly as we read it. What I read astonished me:

Apprentices of the S.A.S.D.,

We have heard of the plight now afflicting many of our kind, and we know of a certain cure. In the Dragon Master's chamber in the city of London are two great treasures: a book and a chalice. In the first there is an ancient recipe; mixed within the other, it provides a remedy for all ills, however foul. You must retrieve them. You, the Master's apprentices, are the only ones we trust with this task. Your mission must be kept secret, lest others attempt to stop you. The way to the chamber is hidden. The dragon chick must light it. Go with dragon speed!

Underneath the message was the mark of a dragon's foreclaw with a very distinctive, heart-shaped pad in the centre. But unlike the writing, this did not vanish.

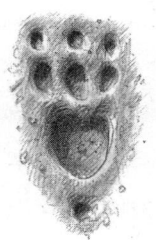

Chapter VI
A Secret Mission

*Apart from the case of the gregarious — and careful — gargouille,
dragons should avoid trips to human cities, whatever draws them.*
— Liber Draconis, 'Humanology:
Notes on Our Unscaly Friends'

Unsurprisingly, no matter what the message said,
Mademoiselle Gamay expressed deep misgivings
about our going on a secret mission to London without
Dr. Drake's say-so. She was particularly unhappy about our
taking Torcher with us — a thing that all of us knew to be
utterly forbidden. However, she recognised the distinctive
mark of the dragon's foreclaw and knew the message to be
a genuine communication from the Society of Dragons.
Moreover, we convinced her that Darcy was almost old
enough to be counted as an adult, and this went some way
to reassuring her that all would be well. So the next
morning found Beatrice, Darcy, Nia and me — along with
Torcher, whom we had concealed in the largest carpet-bag

Mademoiselle Gamay could find — boarding a train headed for Waterloo Station in London. From there, we decided we would make our way on foot to Dr. Drake's Dragonalia — the headquarters of the Secret and Ancient Society of Dragonologists — in Wyvern Way. For the first part of our journey, we had an entire railway compartment to ourselves and had placed the carpet-bag on the floor in front of us, where we could keep an eye on it. Shortly before we left, we had fed Torcher a large meal of fresh meat from the butcher, which we hoped would put him to sleep, but, so far, he was still awake. In order to keep him quiet, we had allowed him to keep Mademoiselle Gamay's earring and Mr. Tibbs's pocket watch, which was now, in any case, a pale, dented shadow of its former self.

In another bag was the lunch Mademoiselle Gamay had prepared for us: sandwiches and some lemonade, as well as some pieces of roast chicken, which we could use to pacify Torcher, should he make a nuisance of himself. We all knew that, were he to be discovered, it would be an absolute disaster.

As the train set off, we discussed what we were going to do when we arrived at Wyvern Way.

"Our mission has to stay secret, so if anyone

questions us, we can say that we have brought Nia up to see Dr. Drake's Dragonalia," said Beatrice. "We'd have done that sooner or later, anyway."

"Yes," said Nia. "That will be just fine, so long as Torcher doesn't give us away."

"As I see it," said Beatrice, "there are two main difficulties. First, we have to get past Mr. Flyte, who will be behind the counter at Dr. Drake's shop. Then we need to find this hidden chamber without being spotted."

"I've never heard of any hidden chamber," said Darcy, "but I know where the Dragon Master's *office* is. And Mademoiselle Gamay has given me Dr. Drake's keys."

He held them up.

"And I think I can help with getting past that Mr. Flyte," said Nia.

"How's that?" I asked.

"Well, I've never met him before, so he won't recognise me, as he would you. I'll keep him talking while you three sneak down the stairs. I'll meet you out front afterwards."

"Good plan," said Beatrice.

Just then, the train pulled into a station, and a crowd of people got on.

"Might we?" said a large, red-faced lady, opening the door of our compartment.

"Of course," said Darcy, though he looked anxiously at the carpet-bag at the same time.

The lady, who was wearing tortoiseshell spectacles and a voluminous green dress, bustled in, followed by the rest of her family: a tall, thin man with sharp elbows, a chubby boy of our own age, who was carrying a large bag of mint humbugs, and a girl of six or seven who had a silver brooch in the shape of a butterfly pinned to the front of her jacket. They squeezed alongside us on the benches. The lady, who was sitting next to me, prodded the carpet-bag with her toe in order to move it out of her way. Torcher gave a very slight growl.

The woman looked at the bag and then frowned at me.

"I didn't know they allowed pets on trains, Hector," she said, turning to her husband.

"Is it a dog or a cat?" the man asked Darcy.

"It must be a cat," said the boy before Darcy could answer, stuffing another mint into his mouth as he spoke, "because I can smell it. Phew, it smells as if it hasn't been washed in weeks."

"If you don't like cats, you can always choose another

compartment," said Nia.

The woman opened her mouth as if to speak, then turned to her husband again. "Well? Are you just going to sit there and let them insult us like that?"

But just then, the girl, who had been watching her brother stuff mint after mint into his mouth, began clamouring for one. "I want a mint. I want a mint," she said, leaning over towards him to grab the bag. "Give me one now!"

The boy tried to move the bag out of her reach, but he wasn't quick enough. The bag tore, and mints showered across the carriage. Two landed in my lap, and one fell into the carpet-bag. I prayed that Torcher wouldn't eat it and get the hiccups. Meanwhile, the boy tried to rescue all the mints he could as the girl scrambled after the ones that had fallen on the floor. To do so, she had to reach right over the carpet-bag.

To my horror, I noticed that when she sat up again, her butterfly brooch was missing.

"Tickets, please!" said the guard, stepping into the compartment, just as I heard a rustling noise coming from the carpet-bag. I took a piece of chicken and dropped it through the opening. The woman saw me and glared.

We handed the guard our tickets, and he looked at them and moved on down the train. I breathed a sigh of relief.

"I saw that," said the woman. "Feeding a cat on the train. Disgusting, disgusting, disgusting."

Nia looked as though she was going to say something, but was stopped by the sound of a very distinct hiccup. I coughed loudly, trying to cover up Torcher's noise, and prayed that he didn't follow it up with a spot of fire-breathing.

"Disgusting," repeated the woman. "I've half a mind to have that animal thrown off the train at the next stop." Fortunately, she showed no sign of carrying out her threat but settled back into her seat, prodding me with her elbows.

I looked down at the carpet-bag. To my horror, a faint wisp of smoke was coming out of the top!

Beatrice, who was sitting on the other side of me, had seen it too.

There was a sound of hiccupping again, and this time a trail of smoke wafted quite clearly out of the top of the bag, accompanied by the unmistakable aroma of roast chicken.

The woman looked at us in horror. Then she turned

to her husband.

"Hector, report these children to the guard immediately. They are definitely up to no good."

"What have you got in that bag?" said the man. "It's not a cat at all, is it?"

"Yes, it's just a cat," I said. "We've rescued him from a fire, and now we're taking him to a special veterinarian in London."

I looked out of the window and saw Big Ben coming into view across the river. We were very nearly there! If only we could get off the train before Torcher burned it down!

"It isn't a cat, actually. It's a lizard," said the boy. "I can see its tail. Look."

I barely contained a gasp as I saw that Torcher's tail was hanging out of the back of the bag.

"Yes, well, that scaly bit's just fire damage," I stammered, motioning to the others to get up. Beatrice picked up Torcher's bag, and we all began moving towards the door.

"Brooch!" screamed the girl, realising for the first time that it was missing. "Someone's stolen my brooch!"

The man stood up just as the train pulled into Waterloo Station.

"I think they're thieves!" he said.

Nia was scrambling for the door handle. The woman began to scream.

"Go!" said Darcy.

Nia threw open the carriage door. Beatrice popped her hand into Torcher's bag, grabbed the brooch, and flung it at the man. Then we fled as fast as we could, down the corridor and off the train. We ran along the platform and onto the wide, curved concourse of Waterloo Station. In fact, we did not stop running until we had gone down to the river, all the way along the embankment and across the bridge, arriving in Trafalgar Square at the bottom of St. Martin's Lane, where we paused to get our breath back. A woman approached us.

"Would you like to buy some lucky heather, my love?" she said.

"No," said Beatrice. "We would not." She said it so forcefully that the woman backed off sharply.

"I was only asking," she said.

※

We approached the entrance to Wyvern Way and put our plan into action. Nia gave us a thumbs-up, and then rounded the corner, heading towards the shop. We waited for ten minutes and then followed her. We peered in a corner of the window. Although it was difficult to make out much of what was inside, what with all of the dragon-related paraphernalia in the window, we could see that Nia had got Mr. Flyte over to the other side of the shop, where she was gesticulating at some dragon models and shouting. Mr. Flyte was doing his best to calm her down. Confident that we wouldn't be seen, we slipped in through the door and hastened over to the back of the shop, where we ducked down behind the sales counter. Nia was putting on quite a display.

"Perhaps if you could come back with your father?" said Mr. Flyte.

"My daddy doesn't know I brought them here from Texas," said Nia. "They are his dragon rodeo trophies. I wasn't supposed to bring them. They were stolen from my hotel room, and now they're right there on that shelf! A boy at my hotel said that I could find them here. My daddy will be angrier than a mule that's backed into a hornet's nest! You won't want to have to deal with him, for sure."

"But those models have been in the shop for some time," said Mr. Flyte with a puzzled air. "They cannot be the same ones, my dear."

"Then I'll have to come back with a posse from the Embassy!" shouted Nia. "We'll see justice done here. I am a Texan! You won't get away with this!"

"I rather think you ought to do just that," said Mr. Flyte.

"You just watch me and see if I don't," said Nia. "That boy also said that downstairs there is some sort of secret animal society, and that if you wouldn't give me my statues back, then I should tell you that I would fetch one of your policemen and report you for the maltreatment of lizards..."

We didn't hear anything more, for we had opened the door behind the counter that led down to the headquarters of the Secret and Ancient Society of Dragonologists. I was carrying Torcher's bag, so I moved extra slowly so as not to disturb him. We didn't want him making a racket now! When we reached the bottom of the stairs, Darcy motioned for us to follow him down the hallway. On the left was the door to the dragonological laboratory, where I had first met Torcher's elder brother, Scorcher. At the end of the hall lay a pair of double doors. We looked behind us, but there did not seem to be anyone about, so Darcy gently pushed them open, and we followed him into a large marble hall with a statue of a dragon in its centre. The room was lit by gas lamps around the edge.

"Let's be careful," whispered Darcy. "If the lights are on, there must be someone about."

"Who?" I asked.

"Emery, perhaps, or maybe Mr. Tibbs or Lord Chiddingfold," said Darcy. "Or maybe one of the other members. There are quite a few, you know."

"Where is the Dragon Master's office?" whispered Beatrice. "We must be quick. Nia won't be able to hold Mr. Flyte's attention forever."

"I think we need to go down the corridor that's behind that door over there," said Darcy, pointing to an elaborately carved door on the far side of the room. "Do you see? It's marked with a *D*-rune."

And sure enough, it was.

"Then let's go!" I said.

We crept over to the other side of the room and tried the door — it was unlocked. We entered the pitch-black hallway beyond. Darcy took out a candle that we had brought and lit it with a match. The flare of the match caused Torcher to stir. I opened the bag and hushed him with another piece of chicken.

"It won't be long, little dragon," I said. "But you've

got to stay quiet and help us to find the things that Dr. Drake needs."

Torcher looked up at me as if he understood and then started eating his chicken.

I looked around. We were in a long, dark, mahogany-panelled corridor. After a short distance I noticed a series of portraits hanging on the walls: on the right were pictures of men and women, and on the left, pictures of some very imposing-looking dragons. There were fewer portraits of dragons, and they were longer and larger. The further we went along the corridor, the more antiquated the style of the portraits became.

"These must be the Dragon Masters!" I said. "Look — this last one has to be Ebenezer Crook."

"And these will be the members of the Society of Dragons!" said Beatrice. "But we don't have time to look at them now. Where is the Dragon Master's office?"

"I think it's that one at the very end," said Darcy.

Going along the corridor, we passed a few bookshelves and pieces of furniture. Then, to our horror, we saw a light coming from behind one of the doors about halfway down.

"That's the Society library," said Darcy. "And there's someone in there."

"I've got a nasty feeling—" I began, just as the door started to swing open.

Darcy snuffed out the candle at once, and we backed against the wall beside a large bookcase. Mr. Tibbs stuck his head out from the open doorway and peered up the corridor into the darkness.

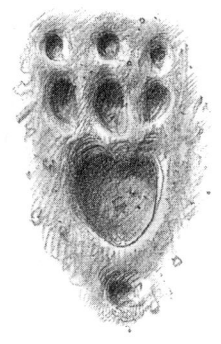

Chapter VII
THE DRAGON MASTER'S OFFICE

If you must communicate with humans, don't make it too easy.

They value a challenge.

— Liber Draconis, 'Humanology:

Notes on Our Unscaly Friends'

"I'm sure I heard something!" said Mr. Tibbs.

Beatrice stifled a gasp. I could feel Torcher stiffen.

Another man stepped out into the corridor. It was Lord Chiddingfold.

"Now, Tibbs," he said. "Calm down. There is no one else here."

There was a pause, then Mr. Tibbs said, "Well, Minister, we shall see. I am almost sure that I can smell a very distinct and vaguely familiar *smell*."

Beatrice and I had grown so used to the sulphurous odour Torcher gave out that we didn't even notice it. I tried to hold the top of the bag shut and hoped the dragon chick would keep quiet.

Lord Chiddingfold ushered Mr. Tibbs back into the library and shut the door behind them. I gave a sigh of relief.

"Do you think we should tell them why we're here?" whispered Beatrice.

"No," replied Darcy, "The dragons told us not to tell *anyone*, them included!"

We waited a few more minutes before we groped our way onwards down the corridor in near total darkness.

"I think this is the door to the Dragon Master's office," whispered Darcy, stopping beside a door carved with a huge curved dragon. "I just need to find the right key to open it."

Meanwhile, Torcher was getting restless — he butted his snout up against the opening of the bag.

"It won't be long now, little dragon!" I whispered to him. But Torcher had had enough. He let out a muffled but unmistakable roar.

Darcy opened the door just in time and pulled Beatrice and me into the room as the library door opened again. He shut the door and fumbled with Dr. Drake's keys in an effort to lock it behind us.

"I *knew* it!" cried Mr. Tibbs from the corridor. "There *is* someone out there, and they've got a dragon with them!"

"A dragon?" exclaimed Lord Chiddingfold. "But everyone knows that's completely forbidden!"

We heard loud steps coming down the corridor towards us. Darcy just managed to turn the key in the lock before someone grabbed the handle on the other side.

"Open up!" said Mr. Tibbs, rattling the door handle. "Or you'll be in even more trouble than you're in already."

We did not reply.

"Who do you think it is?" asked Lord Chiddingfold.

"I don't know," said Mr. Tibbs. "But it smells like that dragon chick from Castle Drake!"

"Let's get the keys from Mr. Flyte," said Lord Chiddingfold.

The next thing we heard was Lord Chiddingfold and Mr. Tibbs going back up the corridor. I hoped that Nia had left by now. There was a small flash as Darcy struck another match and relit the candle. I looked around. We were in a large, square room with one main item of furniture: an enormous and very ancient black desk with dragons carved into it. On it were a few books, and beside it was a black, wooden chair, carved in the shape of a dragon. On each wall of the room hung a different tapestry depicting a famous scene from dragonological history. I recognised two of them from our lessons: Merlin freeing the dragons beneath Dinas Emrys and Fu Hsi meeting the dragon from the Yellow River. The other two were unfamiliar. One showed a Crusader knight presenting a large gem to a white dragon, while the other showed a woman with a sword protecting a baby dragon from a group of medieval soldiers. I put down the carpet-bag and let Torcher out. He stretched and began sniffing about.

I glanced at the titles of the books on the table. They were: *The History of the Secret and Ancient Society of Dragonologists, 1281 to 1842*, *The Ancient History of Dragons*, and *Words of the Dragon Masters – Dragonological Wisdom Through the Ages*.

Under normal circumstances I would have loved to look through those books, but there was no time for that now.

"Have you found anything?" asked Darcy as he peered along the cracks in the stone floor.

"There are some books over here," I said.

Beatrice was rummaging behind the tapestries.

"I can't see anything that looks like a chalice," she said. "Do you think that Mr. Tibbs or Lord Chiddingfold could have come in here and taken it? If so, we're on a wild goose chase."

"I'm not sure we're in the right place yet," said Darcy. "This is the Dragon Master's office. But the message said that the treasures are in the Dragon Master's *chamber*."

"It also said *The way to the chamber is hidden. The dragon chick must light it,*" I added.

"But how do we get Torcher to do that?" said Beatrice.

"I don't know," I said.

But then we noticed that the baby dragon was motionless, staring intently at one of the tapestries. He hiccupped loudly.

"He's going to breathe fire!" cried Darcy.

"Perhaps *this* is how he'll light the way!" exclaimed Beatrice.

Torcher blew out a thin stream of blue flame.
Then, as its glare lit up the tapestry of Merlin, I noticed
something shining. It was woven into the picture, and
I recognised it at once from our dragonology lessons.
It was a dragon rune, hidden along the length of
Merlin's wand. I looked at the tapestry more closely. On
the tail of the red dragon in the same picture, I could see
another rune.

I pointed them out to Darcy and Beatrice.

"There's an *S*-rune and a *T*-rune. I think they are part
of some kind of hidden message," I said.

"What can it mean?" said Beatrice. "Do you think
there are more? Look — isn't that a *W*-rune on the white
dragon's tail?" And indeed, there was a rune, this one
much larger than the others.

"And there's an *E*-rune," I said, pointing to one hidden
in the folds of Merlin's sleeve.

"But what do they mean?" said Beatrice.

"Let's try reading them left to right," I suggested.

"Of course," said Beatrice. " *W-E-S-T*. West. Maybe
the four tapestries mark the points of the compass!"

But Darcy had already taken Torcher to breathe fire
over the other tapestries, and soon we had found a
message made up of four words: *WEST, FIRE, WALL*

and *SHOW*.

"West fire wall show?" I said. "It doesn't make any sense. Are you sure we haven't missed something?"

"No," said Beatrice. "You're reading the words in the wrong order — that's all. It says, 'Show fire west wall'. But which is the west wall?"

"The one with *WEST* on it?" I suggested sarcastically.

Quickly, Darcy pulled back the tapestry and ran the candle over the wall. We waited for a second, but nothing happened.

"Let's try Torcher again," I suggested.

"Of course!" exclaimed Beatrice.

But when Beatrice put Torcher down and pointed him in the direction of the wall, he showed no sign of repeating his attempts to breathe fire.

We heard steps approaching in the corridor.

"Quick! Tickle him under the chin!" I whispered as loudly as I dared.

As Beatrice did as I'd suggested the footsteps stopped outside the door. Torcher hiccupped, then stretched his head back and blew out a stream of flame. A single image of a dragon's footprint became illuminated on the wall in front of him.

"What do we do now?" hissed Beatrice.

"I don't know — push it?" I whispered back.

Beatrice went over to the wall and placed her hand over the footprint.

"Nothing's happening," she said. But then she spread out her fingers to match the position of the claw marks and pushed again. There was a click, and part of the wall slid open to reveal a dark corridor.

Behind us, we could hear a key being inserted into the lock.

"Let's go!" said Darcy, grabbing Torcher's bag. I picked up Torcher, and we squeezed through the gap and down a narrow set of ancient-looking stone steps. As soon as Beatrice released her hand from the dragon's footprint, the wall started to close. She just made it through before we heard the door in the room behind us burst open and Mr. Tibbs's voice cry, "What the devil...?"

Then the opening shut completely, and we could hear no more.

As we arrived, gasping, at the bottom of the staircase, we found another door, which led into a very strange room indeed.

Chapter VIII
LIBER DRACONIS

*As I made humans my chief area of study, most of the chapters in this
book have something to do with them.*
— Liber Draconis, 'Introduction'

The first thing I noticed about the chamber in which
we found ourselves was that it was extremely old.
There was a series of curved arches along the sides and
the remains of a tunnel that had been bricked up at one
end, but the most amazing thing was that the walls
shimmered with what seemed to be a fine coating of
ancient dragon dust, a precious and magical commodity
that, we had learned, came from the breath of a nesting
dragon. Moreover, quite apart from the dancing light
cast by our candle, the room was filled with a red glow,
which gave it the appearance of a wizard's workshop.

There was all manner of strange equipment strewn
around the place, a pile of what seemed to be eight or
nine pieces of sloughed-off dragon skin and, along one

wall, a large display cabinet, which had several drawers underneath. I opened one to find a pile of red feathers. Another drawer contained nothing but fine ash, while a third was filled to the top with sparkling gems, which I guessed could only have come from a dragon's hoard.

Torcher's eyes lit up when he saw the gems, and he wriggled out of my grasp and jumped down onto the floor, darting towards the cabinet. But before he could get at the gems, something else caught his attention. He scampered over to the other side of the room and stood in front of what looked like a medieval monk's lectern.

A small book was resting on it, and fixed in the middle of the book's cover was an enormous red jewel.

I suddenly realised that the strange glow in the room was coming from this very gem. Then I noticed that next to the book was an ancient-looking goblet that seemed strangely familiar.

"Look, everyone!" I called out. "I think I've found what we're after."

"Isn't that book one of the treasures of the S.A.S.D.?" asked Beatrice. "*Liber Draconis*, I think it's called. I recognise it from a picture I saw in Dr. Drake's study. But I didn't think it was a *recipe* book."

"If it is *Liber Draconis*," said Darcy, "only a Dragon Master is allowed to know what it contains, and it is written in Dragonish."

Gently I lifted the book's cover. It was made out of some sort of red leather, and around the outside of the gem was the embossed circular image of a dragon. There was no title and, as I opened it, I was surprised to find that the pages inside were empty.

"It don't think this can be *Liber Draconis*," I said. "It's blank inside."

"What about the goblet?" said Darcy, pointing to the cup. "Maybe that's the chalice we're looking for. Could it be Saint Petroc's Chalice?"

"Of course!" said Beatrice. "If I remember rightly, Saint Petroc's Chalice is another of the S.A.S.D.'s ancient treasures, which bears the names of the ingredients of a cure for sick dragons around its rim. The ingredients must be mixed in the cup itself. It makes perfect sense."

"You're right!" said Darcy. "It must be Saint Petroc's Chalice. I can see some sort of writing around the edge. There are four words: *ANTIMONIUM, SULPHUR, AQUA,* and *VERBENA*. They must be in Latin or something."

"Look at Torcher!" I said.

The dragon chick was circling the lectern as though working out what to do. Then, before any of us could stop him, he leaped up, flapping his wings furiously. He knocked the book with his tail and it fell to the floor, where he stood over it, gazing intently into the gem.

I went to take the book from him, but Beatrice held me back.

"Be careful," she said.

"Is he becoming hypnotised?" I asked.

"I don't know," she replied. "Let's see what he does."

Torcher continued to stare into the gem for some time. Then he backed away from it and hiccupped.

"Oh, no!" exclaimed Beatrice.

We both leaped forwards. But it was too late. Before we could reach him, Torcher opened his mouth and breathed out a thin jet of flame. It lasted only a few seconds, but for that brief moment, the cover of the book was bathed in blue fire. We waited for it to begin to crackle and burn, but instead the gem glowed even more brightly.

"Look!" said Beatrice.

Before our eyes the image of a three-dimensional dragon's head formed inside the gem, while some red, gothic letters, which must have been written in ink that was sensitive to dragon flame, appeared on the cover. They read: *LIBER DRACONIS.*

"Torcher," I said, "you're a marvel."

Torcher looked pleased with himself. He trotted over to the book and curled up next to it. As he did so, the lettering began to fade, and the dragon's-head image disappeared.

"I think it's time to go," said Beatrice.

I tried to pick Torcher up, but he wasn't very happy about it. In fact, he wriggled out of my grip, hopped down next to *Liber Draconis*, and curled up again.

Beatrice stepped forwards and picked up both Torcher and the book.

"Good idea!" I said. "But hang on a moment."

I took a couple of pieces of sloughed-off skin and placed them at the bottom of the carpet-bag.

"Just in case there's any more fire breathing," I said.

Gently Beatrice put both Torcher and the book into the bag, and I loosely did up the straps. Meanwhile, Darcy took off his jacket and used it to wrap up the chalice.

"Now that we have the treasures, let's see if there's another way out," said Darcy.

On the other side of the room was a door similar to the one we had entered by. We opened it and found another set of stairs going up.

"Let's go," said Beatrice. "We need to find Nia."

We headed up the stairs together and soon found ourselves in a corridor so low that we had to stoop. At the end, it opened out to reveal an ordinary-sized door.

Darcy examined it by the light of the candle. "It looks easy to open from this side," he said. "I wonder if this corridor was designed so that the Dragon Master could escape danger in times of need."

"We'll soon find out," said Beatrice. "Can you hear anything on the other side?"

Darcy put his ear to the door.

"It sounds like the street outside," he said. "Get ready."

Darcy unlatched the door, and we stepped out into a

narrow alley that ran between two of the shops next to Dr. Drake's Dragonalia. It was blocked off at one end so, shutting the door behind us, we headed towards Wyvern Way.

"Wait a minute," muttered Beatrice. "Who's that?"

My eyes followed Beatrice's gaze. There was a man in a tattered black jacket standing against the wall at the end of the alley. He had been peering round the wall, presumably watching the front of Dr. Drake's shop. But now he turned to look directly at us.

"Quick!" I exclaimed. "Let's get back inside!"

Darcy tried to open the door again, but there was no handle. The man began to advance towards us menacingly, so that he was entirely blocking the alleyway. There was no way out. He leaned over us, gestured towards the bag and hissed, "I smell *dragons*!"

Beatrice looked back at him.

"I don't know what you're talking about," she replied.

"You've got a dragon in that bag," said the man in a strong cockney accent. "I like dragons. I sell them for lots and lots of money."

"Get away from us!" said Darcy.

"Oh, no," said the man, grinning through a mouthful of yellow teeth. "Not until you give me that bag."

We had backed away as far as we could.

The man lifted up the corner of his black jacket to show that he was carrying a pistol.

"Now, put it down like sensible children," he said. "I'm sure Dr. Drake has taught you always to do as you are told."

Slowly I placed the carpet-bag on the floor.

"Stay back," he said.

He reached down and undid the top of the bag. Torcher's snout poked out. There was a loud hiccup.

"Aww, look, it's a little baby dragon," began the man. "And it's got a book. What is it? Bedtime stories for dragon chicks?"

Suddenly, a jet of blue flame streaked towards him, making the man jump backwards and cover his face.

"Run!" shouted Beatrice.

As quickly as I could, I picked up the bag, pushed past the man and ran up the alley into Wyvern Way. Just at that very moment, a black hansom cab came tearing towards us from the direction of the Seven Dials.

"Look!" said Beatrice. "It must be Lord—"

But the door of the cab opened, and Nia Hayes stuck out her head.

"Well?" she said. "What are you folks waiting for?"

We leaped into the cab, and Nia shouted, "Go, driver! Giddy up! Yah!"

As we sped away down St. Martin's Lane, I turned around to see the man in the black jacket shaking his fist at us.

Chapter IX
An Unexpected Journey

*Try not to give rides unless it is really necessary,
or you will find young humans begging for them incessantly.*
— Liber Draconis, 'The Humanology Handbook'

Mademoiselle Gamay was extremely relieved when we arrived back at Castle Drake and told her everything that had taken place.

"*Mon Dieu!* What a lucky escape!" she said. "But what on earth was that man doing there?"

"Do you have any idea who he was?" I asked.

"I don't," she replied.

"Well, at least he didn't recognise *Liber Draconis,*" said Beatrice. "And he didn't get a chance to see Saint Petroc's Chalice, either."

"But what should we do now?" I asked.

"We must wait, I suppose," said Beatrice. "Until we receive word from the Society of Dragons. Or until Panthéon pays us a visit."

"But where shall we keep the treasures in the meantime?" I said. "They need to be somewhere pretty secure."

"Why don't we keep them with Torcher?" said Beatrice. "I'm sure he'll be able to protect them, won't you, little one?"

We agreed that Torcher would make an excellent guardian for the treasures, but all the same, Mademoiselle Gamay found us a thick chain and an extremely heavy padlock to put on the coal-shed door before we went to bed that night.

The next day I awoke in a cold sweat. I could hear barking coming from the driveway at the front of Castle Drake and angry shouting from downstairs. I quickly pulled on my clothes and found Beatrice and Nia standing on the upstairs landing, looking over the banisters with worried expressions. Downstairs, I could see Mademoiselle Gamay in the grip of two burly policemen. In front of her was a man dressed in the uniform of a police inspector. But, unusually, his cape was decidedly tatty and crumpled, and the big buttons down the front of his jacket were dull and rusty.

"It's him!" whispered Beatrice.

"Who?" I whispered back.

"The man from the alley. He's pretending to be a policeman, but there's no mistaking him."

"Do you think he followed us?"

"He must have."

"I refuse to be arrested!" cried Mademoiselle Gamay to the man. "I have not done anything wrong."

"Haven't done anything wrong indeed!" said the man with a sneer that revealed the same yellow teeth I had seen less than twenty-four hours previously. "Well, let me tell you that *you*, madam, are under arrest as a dubious alien who is also suspected of illegal dealings with rare and unusual lizards."

"What on earth are you talking about?" said Mademoiselle Gamay. "What sort of lizards?"

"Dragons, madam," said the man. "Big ones. And small ones. And middle-sized ones too. In fact, offences on numerous occasions."

"I don't know what you're talking about," cried Mademoiselle Gamay. "It's true that we have a pet cat that burned its tail, but —"

"Silence!" shouted the man. "Put her in the cart with the boy," he ordered his companion, "and search the house for the others! Use the dogs if you have to.

And bring me any evidence you find, particularly anything that looks valuable."

"They're taking her away!" I whispered. "And they must have Darcy too. We're going to be next, if we don't do something!"

"Well, I'll be darned if I'll let those big bullies take Torcher or the treasures," whispered Nia defiantly. "You and Beatrice go get them and hide out in the forest! Try to get a message to the Society of Dragons."

"What about you?" I said.

"I'm going to distract them," said Nia. "Now, go!"

And with that, she began to descend the stairs.

Nia certainly had guts. She ran straight up to the bigger of the two fake policemen and poked his chest with her finger.

"Look here, mister," she said. "You don't look much like an officer of the law to me. You bring that nice French lady back. And you get out of this here house right *now*."

"Hey, Shadwell!" cried the big fake policeman to the man with yellow teeth. "I've got one of the kids right here."

"Then put her in the cart and find the others," came the reply.

"We need to get outside before they start searching up here," Beatrice said to me.

"There's a tree outside your dormitory window," I said. "Do you think we can climb down that?"

"It's worth a try," said Beatrice.

We climbed onto the window ledge and from there into the tree. It wasn't difficult to climb down, except for the last four feet or so, which we had to jump.

We ran to the coal shed and unlocked it.

Beatrice picked up Torcher, who held on tightly to *Liber Draconis* with his claws.

"It seems as if he and that book are inseparable," I said as I picked up Saint Petroc's Chalice.

We crept as quickly and as quietly as we could towards the gate at the far end of the garden. We had nearly reached it when a shout went up from inside the house, followed by the sound of furious barking.

"Oh, no," said Beatrice. "I think they've seen us. Run!"

"Where shall we go?" I cried.

"Let's try crossing over the forest streams," said Beatrice. "It might put the dogs off the scent."

Torcher kept looking back and roaring as we headed down a sandy bank and over the first of the streams, then back up again past a patch of purple gloop that showed that Weasel had been around.

"If only we could get to Weasel," I said. "Would that scare the dogs off?"

"No," said Beatrice. "Don't you remember what happened with Torcher? Unless Weasel's hungry, it's just as likely that she would be scared of the dogs."

"What about Jamal?"

"We mustn't let them find Jamal. He said he was a dragon dealer, remember," cried Beatrice.

We ran onwards and came to the second of the two streams. But as we bolted down the steep bank to cross it, two men burst out of the undergrowth behind us. One of them was holding two dogs on a chain. The dogs were almost dragging their master along behind them in their eagerness to get at us.

"There they are!" the man with the dogs cried. "Get them, Cruncher! Hold them fast, Fang!"

He released the dogs, and they bounded towards us, barking horribly and baring their teeth.

"We've got to surrender!" I shouted. "We don't have any other choice. Those dogs are going to—"

But just as the first dog was almost upon us, a mighty roar boomed through the forest, and the dogs stopped dead in their tracks. Their menacing barks turned to yowls of fright as they turned tail and ran back towards the men who were following us.

"It's Jamal!" cried Beatrice. "He's come to rescue us!"

And it was true. There, plunging through the undergrowth, was Jamal.

"Shumul algrrrri!" he said. *"Shumul algrrrri!"*

He bent his knees and turned round.

The men had put the chains back on the dogs and were advancing towards us once more, slowed by their whimpering hounds, which they now had to drag along behind them.

"Shumul algrrrrri," repeated Jamal, and he nudged me with his snout.

"Jamal wants us to climb onto his back," I said in sudden realisation. "He's going to fly us to safety! Good old Jamal!"

"What?" said Beatrice, shooting me a doubtful look.

"Quick! Climb up," I said to Beatrice. "Jamal never flies very far. We'll be safe. Or at least safer than we are here."

Beatrice passed Torcher to me and clambered up onto Jamal's back. I passed Torcher up to her and then swung up behind her, clutching the chalice.

As soon as we were on, Jamal took one step, two

steps, and a third, then lifted himself into the sky with a little more effort than usual, given his three passengers. Below us, the men broke into a run, but it was too late — we were out of their clutches.

"Phew, that was close!" I said.

"As long as Jamal doesn't decide to go for a very short flight and just return to where he picked us up," said Beatrice.

We headed up over the trees of St. Leonard's Forest and high into the air. Soon we were far enough away from Castle Drake for me to feel safe.

"I'm going to try to command Jamal to go down now," I said.

"How do you do that?" asked Beatrice.

"Well, I remember the word Darcy used to make him land. I just hope he understands me." Then I shouted at Jamal as loudly as I could,

"*Keramabak! Keramabak!*"

But Jamal ignored me and kept flying.

"*KERAMABAK!*" I yelled, but Jamal showed no sign of slowing down. He wheeled in an arc and turned south. Far away, I could see the English Channel glinting through a gap in the range of hills known as the South Downs. I gripped Jamal as tightly as I could.

"Where in the world is he going?"

"Where in the world is he going?" shouted Beatrice.

I didn't need to answer, because Jamal answered for me. *"Panteoo!"* he roared. *"Shumul algrrrri yaryar Panteoo!"*

"Panthéon?" shouted Beatrice. "But doesn't Panthéon live in Paris?"

"Yes!" I shouted back. "So unless they've arranged a rendezvous somewhere else, I imagine that's where we're heading."

"But how does he know the way?" she cried.

"Perhaps Panthéon showed him!" I shouted.

As we flew over the South Downs, I heard shouts from below. Two children, a girl and a boy, were walking their dog on top of one of the hills. The boy had seen us and was pointing up in great excitement, while the girl looked up in shocked disbelief. *That would have been Beatrice and me a few months ago,* I thought. But just as quickly as I had seen them, we left them behind. Jamal headed straight over the Downs and out across the English Channel. We were flying so high that I could see land on the other side of the sea, which I knew must be France. I wondered how long it would take us to get there and hoped that it wouldn't be too long because, although it was a sunny day, there was a stiff sea breeze and I was already very cold.

"How are you feeling, Bea?" I shouted against the wind.

"Well, it's a bit uncomfortable — you know, *underneath*," Beatrice called back. "But otherwise I'm all right. And Torcher actually seems to be enjoying himself."

Almost as soon as we had mounted Jamal, Torcher had settled down and become very quiet. The thought popped into my head that perhaps it was an instinctive reaction; maybe mother dragons carried their chicks around this way.

"Is there anything we can do, do you think?" I shouted.

"Not until Jamal decides to land," Beatrice called. "Or until Panthéon shows up."

I resigned myself to the flight. It was nothing like the steady flights we had taken on Idraigir, because Jamal's wings were smaller than Idraigir's and he beat them more quickly and with a much jerkier motion. And an experienced dragon like Idraigir was obviously much better at reading air currents. Whenever Jamal encountered pockets of turbulence in the air, he rose and fell dramatically or, more worryingly, tipped sideways.

Soon I was feeling decidedly sick.

It took us less than an hour to reach the coast of France. We flew over a narrow strip of beach and then over farmland separated by small strips of woodland and then a wide river that snaked towards us. Jamal didn't even look down. He simply turned to follow the course of the river and flew onwards.

By the evening, when the sun had sunk low in the sky, I had stopped feeling sick. Instead, I was hungry and thirsty, and I ached all over from sitting on Jamal for so long without any padding. The long journey must have tired the wyvern too, for he was flying much more slowly now. As the sun set, we reached the outskirts of a large city with gas lamps illuminating the boulevards and lights twinkling at the windows.

"I think this might be Paris!" shouted Beatrice.

By now, Jamal's wing beats were becoming laborious, and we had started to lose height. We flew over an area of parkland just outside the city and began to follow the river again. Jamal was flying so low that even in the growing darkness I could make out features on the tops of the tallest buildings. Before us, on an island in the middle of the river, was a large cathedral. It had two square towers with a tall spire behind them.

"Look!" cried Beatrice suddenly.

"Where?" I shouted.

"Right in front of us," she said. "Coming from the cathedral."

I peered into the darkness. A creature that resembled a huge bat had flapped up from the top of one of the towers and was coming towards us.

"It's a gargouille!" said Beatrice.

"Could it be Panthéon?" I asked.

Jamal had seen the gargouille too. He turned towards it.

"Panteoo!" he roared. *"Panteoo!"*

Now many more gargouilles were flapping up from numerous spires and domes and heading in our direction.

"Let's just hope they are Panthéon's friends," I said

"Panteoo!" boomed Jamal.

The first gargouille flew alongside us. It bared its yellow teeth and made a horrid gargling noise.

"Vrrrreschlich boyarrrr!" it shrieked.

"What does that mean?" I asked Beatrice.

"I think it might mean 'go away'," she said.

But Jamal wasn't going away.

"Vrrrreschlich boyarrrr!" roared the incensed gargouille more loudly than before. *"Vrrrreschlich!"*

"I don't think these gargouilles are Panthéon's friends at all," said Beatrice.

Just then, the rogue gargouille turned to Beatrice and me. It gave us a look of utter hatred and stuck out its tongue. Then it flew high above us. Hugging its wings to its body and holding out its claws, it dived towards us at tremendous speed.

"*Gerupthar*, Jamal!" I yelled. "*Gerupthar!*"

Jamal quickly changed direction and flew higher, evading the attacking gargouille. But then another gargouille came diving down, and another and another. Jamal stiffened, gave an angry roar, and poured out a jet of flame.

"Where is Panthéon?" I shouted.

Jamal was doing everything he could to avoid the claws and teeth of the attacking gargouilles as they flew at us. He twisted and turned, and I began to fear that we would fall. Torcher, meanwhile, was doing his best to join in the fight by breathing his own jets of flame at the gargouilles as they passed. By now we had wheeled north and were crossing over the river again. Jamal dropped down towards the bridge that led to the island cathedral.

I guessed that he was going to try to land. Until now,

...it dived towards us at tremendous speed.

our airborne dragon battle had been up high, out of sight of the people of the city, but as we swooped down over the bridge into an area that was well lit by gas lamps, a carriage swerved, a dog barked and a woman screamed. Quickly Jamal flew back up again, and the rogue gargouilles redoubled their attack. Jamal snapped and flapped desperately as he tried to get around them. He dodged a group of three of them, but his wing beats were becoming very laboured. He was tiring rapidly. It could be only a matter of time before one of the gargouilles landed a telling blow, and then, when Jamal was stunned, I was sure the others would be upon us, ripping and tearing and clawing.

We were flying towards a hill with another cathedral at the top. Three more gargouilles rose from its roof.

"They're everywhere!" shouted Beatrice.

Jamal warded off a gargouille on our left with a jet of flame, then swerved to avoid another one on our right. But just as we were passing over a large cemetery, the gargouilles started a new manoeuvre. A huge bunch of them flew towards us at once, closing in to attack from both sides, while others swooped up from underneath us, their bunched fists held out in front of them like battering rams. I could feel the thud, thud, thud as their blows rammed into Jamal. Finally, his strength failed him, and he began to fall from the sky like a stone. In the darkness, the tombs and gravestones of the cemetery rushed towards us.

"Panthéon!" I shouted. And then everything went black.

Chapter X
BERNARD GAMAY

Even gargouilles cannot remember when they first moved
from cliffs to roost on the roofs of Paris.

— Liber Draconis, 'Key Features of Different Dragons'

When I awoke, I felt hungry, thirsty and sore all over. Most of all I had a terrible headache. Sunlight was pouring into the room through a small window. At first my vision was so blurred that all I could see was brightness, but after a while I was able to make out someone sitting on a chair next to my bed.

"Bea?" I whispered.

"Daniel!" cried Beatrice, leaning towards me. "You're awake. Thank goodness! Are you all right?"

She hugged me.

"I think so," I said. "But I have an awful headache. How are you?"

"Aching all over," she admitted.

"Where's Torcher?" I said.

"Oh, he's fine," said Beatrice. She lifted up the quilt and pointed under the bed. I leaned over to see Torcher gazing up at me. Next to him, I could see *Liber Draconis* and the chalice.

"Where are we?" I said.

"We are in the house of Mademoiselle Gamay's brother, Bernard," she said. "It is also the headquarters of the French Dragonological Society. Bernard helped Panthéon to rescue us from the cemetery last night, and he brought us here. I was able to walk, but he had to carry you because you were unconscious. Apparently, Panthéon told him Jamal might bring us here if there was trouble, and so Bernard had been keeping an eye out for us with his telescope. He knew the other gargouilles might be a problem."

"And what about Panthéon?"

"Yesterday he went to Castle Drake to see if we had managed to find the treasures. When he found the house empty and Jamal missing, he guessed there had been some kind of trouble and flew back to Paris as fast as he could."

"And is Jamal all right?"

"He was injured, but he is safe," said Beatrice. "We'll go to see him later. But as soon as you feel up to it, we ought to go downstairs and find Monsieur Gamay."

Beatrice gave me a glass of water and some fruit. After I had drunk and eaten, I felt much better. I got out of bed, and we took Torcher and the treasures and went downstairs to find Bernard Gamay waiting for us. He was a short man, and he seemed to have a taste for exotic, oriental-looking clothes, as he was wearing a silk jacket embroidered with *lung* dragons, and a pair of Chinese slippers.

"Daniel!" he exclaimed, holding out his hand. "How are you feeling?"

"Well, I have a headache," I said, taking his hand and shaking it, "but I think I'll survive."

"Thank goodness!" he said. "Well, it is certainly a pleasure to meet Dr. Drake's *protégés*, even if it is in somewhat unfortunate circumstances. My sister, Dominique, has told me all about you. But come, let us sit in my studio. I fear we do not have a great deal of time, and there are things we need to discuss."

We followed Monsieur Gamay into a high-ceilinged room that was flooded with light from windows that ran along one of the walls. Paints, easels, brushes and paintings lay around, and there were pictures and carvings of dragons everywhere. Torcher nosed around them.

"Has Jamal recovered?" asked Beatrice.

"He is still sleeping," said Bernard. "We will visit him presently, but we must be careful. Your arrival may have gone unseen by most of the population of Paris, but it will certainly have been noticed by others."

"We need to speak with Panthéon," I said.

"Of course," said Bernard. "Panthéon has told me about your mission. You are carrying two of the precious treasures of the S.A.S.D., yes? The Society of Dragons told him they would be entrusting you with this most important mission, but no one foresaw that you would be seen by one of Alexandra Gorynytchka's henchmen. You did well to escape his clutches, my young friends. I am afraid my sister was not so fortunate, nor your American guest. They have not been seen since. Only young Darcy managed to get away. He is in London now, staying with

Lord Chiddingfold, and managed to get a message to us telling us what had happened."

"Does Darcy know that we managed to escape with the treasures?" asked Beatrice.

"You will need to speak to Panthéon about that," said Bernard. "But I must warn you that he was injured last night. His right wing is badly torn. Gargouilles heal quickly from their injuries, but it will be some days before Panthéon can fly far."

"What happened?" I asked.

"He — and the gargouilles that are still loyal to him — were trying to protect you."

"But why did the other gargouilles attack us?" I asked.

"Gargouilles — like other dragons — are fiercely protective of their territory. They would never allow an unknown wyvern to enter it unchallenged. And when they saw that Jamal was being ridden by two humans, an attack was inevitable."

"Why?" asked Beatrice.

"These rogue gargouilles detest humans. They loathe the fact that they must sneak around Paris at night, avoiding being seen. There is only one human whom they trust. Miss Gorynytchka came to them with sweet words and many promises. And she told them that their worst enemies were meddlesome dragonologists."

"I'm surprised that the gargouilles do not fear her. Has the news of what she did to the Guardian not spread to Paris?" I said.

"Fear her? No, I should think not. Miss Gorynytchka promised that if they would give her their help, then the day would come when she would allow them to cleanse Paris of humans completely. Panthéon kept them at bay yesterday, but they will attack again tonight if they find out that you and Jamal are still here."

"I think we should see Panthéon at once," said Beatrice.

"He cannot come and see you before dusk," said Bernard. "He is too large to travel around Paris in the daytime. But we shall visit Jamal now."

He disappeared into a large cupboard, then emerged carrying two travelling capes and a sizeable bag.

"You can put the treasures in this bag. And if you both wear the capes," he said, "you may look a little eccentric, but they will help you to hide Torcher. Does he make a nuisance of himself, by the way?"

"I'm afraid so," I said.

"*C'est la vie,*" said Bernard with a smile. "He is young, after all."

We wrapped the treasures in some pieces of cloth and placed them in the bag, then put on the capes, which were much too big for us. I picked up the bag while Beatrice picked up Torcher and held him in her arms under the cloak. Torcher didn't like having his head covered and kept poking around trying to get his nose out.

"Quiet, Torcher!" said Beatrice.

The whole performance looked so funny that I laughed out loud. Beatrice just rolled her eyes.

We followed Bernard out of the house and onto the cobbled street. It was busy, but no one gave us a second glance as Bernard led us a short distance along the street to the gates of a sloping field surrounded by walls and fences. It was a small vineyard.

Bernard opened the gates, and we followed a path around the top of the vineyard to an old stone building. Bernard unlocked the heavy door and pulled it open. Inside, stone steps led down to a large, cool room with a vaulted ceiling and a floor covered with straw. Around the edges of the room were racks stacked with wine barrels. At the far end, I could make out a familiar shape huddled up in the gloom.

"*Voici* Jamal!" said Bernard.

The young wyvern lay stretched out on the straw.

He opened his eyes as soon as we came in. Beatrice and I rushed over to him. He looked up at us and slowly lifted his head.

"*Prrrraisich hoyarrrri,*" he said.

"*Praisich, Shumul,*" I replied, using his Dragonish name.

Torcher hopped down out of Beatrice's arms, ran over to Jamal and curled up next to him. Jamal let out a sigh and lowered his head, closing his eyes again as he did so.

"Is Jamal badly hurt?" I asked.

"No, not badly," said Bernard. "He has a few scratches, nothing more. However, his first long flight has exhausted him, and he needs to sleep. He will wake up soon. You will be surprised how quickly his flight strength will recover."

We stroked Jamal's scaly head.

"Now," said Bernard, "I must leave you for a short while. The Society of Dragons wanted Panthéon to take the book and the chalice to Dr. Drake once you had retrieved them from London. But now that Panthéon is injured, another way must be found. I must therefore go and speak to the French Dragon Master at once."

"Shouldn't we come with you?" said Beatrice.

"I'm afraid that the French Dragon Master prefers his

identity to be kept strictly secret. He is someone very high up in the government, you know. Of course, he may decide to come and see *you*. Meanwhile, you will be quite safe here. I shall not be more than a few hours at most."

Bernard brushed away some of the straw from the floor to reveal a small trapdoor. "Before I go," he continued, "I must tell you that the French Dragonological Society keeps two spare field kits down here in case of emergencies. You can open them and eat some of the food in them if you get hungry before I come back."

And with that, Bernard left.

Once he had gone, Beatrice and I bolted the door from the inside. At first we played with Torcher. He seemed to enjoy scampering around the cellar, running over to check on Jamal every now and then. And so we waited. An hour passed. Torcher curled up by Jamal and went to sleep.

"I'm hungry," said Beatrice.

"Me too," I said. "Let's see what's in those dragonological field kits."

We pulled open the trapdoor Bernard had shown us to reveal a short ladder that led down into a narrow, low-roofed chamber. Alongside the wall were two wooden chests. Inside I found numerous articles, including two large flameproof cloaks, a magnifying glass, a small mirror, two notebooks, bound in what looked like lead or pewter, two pencils, two pairs of goggles, two leather caps, two small haversacks, a piece of shed dragon skin, a camping knife, a small cooking pot, some rope, two blankets, salt and pepper shakers and a large tarpaulin. There was also a small pouch containing a handful of different types of coin, a few gems and two books, which proved to be a pocket atlas of the world and a more detailed atlas of France. The world atlas was particularly interesting, as someone had jotted down brief notes about the sorts of dragon one might encounter in different countries.

"What a collection!" said Beatrice.

"There are no dragon saddles, though." said Beatrice.

"Can you see any food or drink?" I said.

Beatrice indicated two large tin bottles full of water in leather carrying pouches and a box marked *Vivres* that contained food. When we opened it, the food didn't look very appetising, being mainly strips of dried meat and fish, dried beans and dried peppers. In fact, the only thing that looked edible — without cooking or soaking first — was a large box of ship's biscuits.

The biscuits were dry, but we managed to get them down with some water. Then we waited a little longer. Bernard still did not return.

Jamal stirred and woke up. He did not stand, however, but lay quietly looking at us. Outside, the sun began to set and the city gradually grew dark. I was starting to feel quite anxious, and I could see that Beatrice felt the same.

"Wasn't this when Monsieur Gamay said that the gargouilles might attack again?" I asked.

"Only if they know we're still here," said Beatrice. "It was also when he said Panthéon would come to see us. But where is Monsieur Gamay? He should have returned hours ago."

We climbed the steps and looked out of the small window beside the main cellar door, scanning the city skyline. It wasn't long before we saw a familiar shape flying high overhead, heading straight for us.

Panthéon landed in the vineyard and stepped over to the door. His movements were not as smooth as they had been before, and I noticed that he had a huge gash in his right wing that had been stitched back together with what looked like a leather thong. There were signs of cuts and bruises about his face and body as well.

"Poor Panthéon!" exclaimed Beatrice.

The gargouille bowed low. But he did not greet us with his usual grin.

"Praisich boyar!" I said.

"Prrrraisich hoyarrrri," replied Panthéon. He looked around before ducking in through the door.

Jamal stood up at once and came over to greet him. Meanwhile, Torcher ran around and around him, rubbing his back against Panthéon's leg.

"Très bien!" he said. "You have done well, *mes enfants.* Extremely well," he said. "In fact, you could not have done better. The British Society of Dragons would like you to know that they are proud of you for bringing the treasures safely to Paris. But unfortunately our troubles are not yet over."

"Why?" asked Beatrice anxiously. "Is it the other gargouilles? Do they know we are here?"

"No, no," replied Panthéon, "although they too are a concern. No, it is Bernard, I am afraid. He did not arrive for his meeting."

"What?" I exclaimed.

"It is extremely worrying," said Panthéon. "Moreover, it seems that the French Dragon Master has also disappeared. Paris is becoming a dangerous place for dragonologists."

"So what should we do now?" asked Beatrice.

"I have come here to give you further instructions on this very matter," said Panthéon, "instructions that come directly from the Society of Dragons. They were extremely impressed with your abilities during the episode of the Dragon's Eye. They remain extremely impressed with the way in which you have behaved in this recent escapade."

"With Jamal's help," I said.

"And Torcher's," added Beatrice.

"Indeed," said Panthéon. "But now the Society of Dragons requests that you continue to assist them by delivering *Liber Draconis* and Saint Petroc's Chalice to Dr. Ernest Drake. You must fly with Jamal to his original home in East Africa. For there, beyond a lake named Victoria and near the end of a great river known as the Nile, past a wide plain, is a crater named Ngorongoro. There you will find a wyvern called Uwassa. He is a part of the Dragon Express. And you must ride the Dragon Express to Jaisalmer."

"*Shumul algrrrri yaryar Ufrrrrukh!*" said Jamal excitedly.

"But why us?" asked Beatrice.

"The Society chose you to fetch the treasures from London because they trust you above all others. You are the Dragon Master's apprentices, after all. And we dragons have far more regard for the abilities of children than do most adults of your own kind. I once knew a remarkable—"

But Panthéon's story was interrupted by a sudden thud against the cellar door and a low growl from outside. A glance through the window confirmed our worst fears. Six or seven angry-looking gargouilles were massed outside.

"*Sacré bleu!*" cursed Panthéon. "We must be quick. Gather your supplies, children, and get ready to fly. I will use the other door and create a diversion. The moment your exit is clear, you must make your escape."

"But it's impossible," said Beatrice. "We need you to come with us. We can't just fly to Africa on our own. And anyway, we need the secret password for the Dragon Express, don't we?"

"It is in the book," said Panthéon. "You must use dragon fire to find it. There is no time to argue. The Dragon Master needs you. You must leave *now*."

"Sacré bleu!" *cursed Panthéon. "We must be quick."*

Chapter XI
THE FLIGHT FROM PARIS

Like a displaced dragon, the salmon goes back to the place
where it was spawned, thinking nothing of the dangers.
— Liber Draconis, 'Humans and Other Animals'

The thudding and scraping at the door continued as Beatrice and I gathered as much as we could carry from the dragonological field kits, placing the equipment in the two haversacks. Then, using one of the flameproof cloaks as a makeshift saddle, Bea climbed onto Jamal with Torcher and the bag containing the treasures, while I stood by the main door. Panthéon slipped out of another door at the back of the cellar. There was a moment's silence, followed by a loud crash and a tremendous, gurgling roar.

Sure enough, the ensuing flurry of activity outside told us that our plan had worked. The gargouilles had been drawn away by Panthéon.

After checking that the coast was clear, I unlocked the door, flung it open and jumped up onto Jamal to sit in front of Beatrice, my heart thumping wildly.

Jamal stepped forwards onto the dark slopes of the vineyard, ran two or three steps downhill and launched himself into the air. Below, I could hear angry roars coming from the other side of the cellar.

"I hope Panthéon will be all right," I exclaimed.

"Me too," said Beatrice.

But as Jamal's steady wing beats took us further and further from the vineyard and we strained our eyes to catch sight of Panthéon in the gathering dusk, it became clear that our hopes were unfounded. For in the far distance, we saw Panthéon wheeling away from us, surrounded by what seemed to be a flock of enormous bats, while to the south, another, larger group was forming as a mass of dark shapes flitted up from rooftops all over the city.

Jamal flew onwards, over the river and past the great cathedral on the island, until he was flying across the southern part of Paris. I looked back. In the darkness, I could just make out the two groups of gargouilles wheeling and diving, as though trying to outmanoeuvre each other. Then I saw them rush together high in the air like two swarms of demons as battle was joined. Dimly, I saw bright shafts of flame and heard distant roars. I crossed my fingers and silently wished Panthéon luck. And, as the dark of the night enveloped us and Jamal carried us away across France, I realised that Panthéon was not going to catch up with us. We were safe, but we were on our own — and we were heading all the way to Africa.

✻

Jamal flew much further on his second flight than he had done on his first, and we let him carry on until daybreak. By the time the sun rose over the horizon, he seemed to be tiring, which was convenient, since Beatrice and I had both decided that it would be far better to fly at night to lower our risk of being spotted.

"Keramabak! Keramabak!" I called to him, and was relieved when this time he responded, slowing his wing beats in readiness to land.

In front of us was a tall hill with a crater on top that looked like an extinct volcano. Jamal skirted the hill, swooping over a wood on its lower slopes and over farmers' fields in search of a landing site. He spied what to him must have seemed the perfect spot — the lawn of a large house. He did not seem to notice that there was a woman standing in the garden, hanging out washing on a line. Jamal started to descend.

"No, Jamal!" I called. *"Shumul, mai!"*

Jamal beat his wings and flew on until he spotted an alternative. This time it was a clearing in a small copse that had a stream running through it.

"That looks perfect!" I said. *"Keramabak, Shumul!"*

Jamal began to descend again, just as it struck me that Beatrice and I had not experienced landing with him before. And from my memories of seeing him crash-land in St. Leonard's Forest, I did not have high expectations.

"You'd better brace yourself," I said to Beatrice.

When Jamal was about twenty feet from the ground, he stopped beating his wings and we began to drop. When we were about ten feet from the ground, he put his legs out and flapped so as to drop more slowly, but we were still going down pretty fast. He hit the ground in the middle of the clearing, bending his legs up beneath him to cushion the blow, but the jolt threw Beatrice, Torcher and me clean off his back. Beatrice was lucky enough to catch hold of the branch of a small tree, which broke her fall, while Torcher simply put out his wings and glided down to the ground, holding *Liber*

Draconis in his mouth as he did so. I landed upside down in a thornbush.

"Ouch!" I said. "Thanks a lot, Jamal!"

Jamal came over and nuzzled me with his snout, as though he realised that his landing had been far from perfect.

"Hey, you big oaf!" I said. "Get off me!"

Jamal loped to the stream and began to drink noisily. Torcher joined him. When I stood up, I was amazed to find that I did not feel nearly as stiff and sore as I had when we'd arrived in Paris.

"I think we should have something to eat and then set up camp here for the day," said Beatrice as she unpacked the haversacks.

While we nibbled on some ship's biscuits, I dug out the world atlas from Monsieur Gamay's field kit, which I had stuffed in my haversack, and found the pages that depicted France. We decided that the extinct volcano we had seen was probably called Puy de Dôme and that the large town in the distance was Clermont-Ferrand.

Jamal had settled down near us with Torcher next to him. Beatrice and I rested our backs against the wyvern's flank.

"Shall we look for the password now?" said Beatrice.

"Panthéon said that we'd need to use dragon fire to find it in *Liber Draconis*."

"And we can look for the recipe too!" I exclaimed. "The one the Society of Dragons said would cure the dragon sickness."

This seemed like an excellent idea. Torcher was guarding the bag that contained the treasures by sitting across it. Much to his disgust, which he showed by sticking his forked tongue out at me, I gently prised it out from underneath him and took out the book.

"Fire-breathing time, little dragon," I said.

I placed the book a few feet from Torcher. Jamal looked on with interest. Then I tickled the dragon chick under the chin. It was not long before Torcher hiccupped, then blew out a stream of flame that was much stronger than he had produced before.

"Good dragon!" I cried.

The flames lapped around the book, which glowed as the letters on the cover came to life. Using the shed dragon skin to prevent our hands from being burned, we turned the pages.

The first thing that struck me as we opened the book was that it had pictures in it, which I had not expected. There were illustrations of European dragons, rudimentary maps — mostly of medieval Europe, by the look of things — and illustrations of various peoples in different kinds of dress. It looked like some sort of diary, because each entry was preceded by something that looked like a date, but there didn't seem to be any logic to its organisation, since many of the pages were blank, while others were written in different languages and different scripts.

About a third of the way through the diary, we came to a section that was written in a sort of English. It said:

This is an ensample of the Englyssh tonge of Edward Longshanks's reyn as I have founde it. The saynt of Engelond, George, is by repute a sleyer of dragons, and hir king, Edward Longshanks, desired the deths of all the dragons in that kingdom. Yet the Englyssh hath a feloweshipe of serned frends of dragons called dracomancers, who are worthy and wys folk, though secret in alle. Master amonge them hath bene Beatrice Croke, for she holped dragons such as my self against Longshanks and his men and, when alle was ouer, in a depe cauern under flowing water, she hid the means Longshanks had for theyre sleying: the deadlie black powdre and the yellow and red poysons, willing that cauern sealed forever and taking into her cayre twelve mightie treasures and hiding them among those dragons that still liued.

As we finished reading, the lines began to fade.

"That's strange," said Beatrice. "I thought *Liber Draconis* was written by a man called Gildas Magnus, but this sounds as if it was written by a dragon."

"I know," I agreed. "And I'm not sure that finding the password is going to be all that easy. The spelling isn't very good, and there are some words I don't understand at all."

"That's because it's written in old-fashioned English, from hundreds of years ago," explained Beatrice. "I remember Dr. Drake telling us about Beatrice Croke in one of our dragonological history lessons, but I don't remember anything about any poisons being hidden in a cavern."

"Do you really think it could have been written by a dragon?" I asked. "And if it was, why are the entries in all these different languages? And why are there all these blank pages in between?"

"I don't know," said Beatrice. "I just hope we can find the password before we get to Ngorongoro. Otherwise, we'll be in real trouble — and so will all those sick dragons."

But although we spent the rest of the day in the clearing searching through the book, there was no sign of the password, nor of any recipe that could be the cure for dragon sickness, which we so desperately wanted to find.

❋

That evening we set off on Jamal again and flew south. After a few hours, we came to some marshes by the sea, where a great cloud of pink flamingos wheeled up underneath us, frightened by the sight of the wyvern flying overhead. Jamal turned west, following the coast, and then inland, over a small mountain range. It was a clear, cold night, and we were very glad indeed of the capes Bernard had given us. As dawn was breaking, we arrived on the other side of the mountains and Jamal descended onto a rocky peninsula. He landed on a low slope by a waterfall, scaring a flock of goats in the process. Landing on a slope seemed to be easier for him than alighting on a flat piece of ground, and this time we were not thrown off but managed to dismount in a much more dignified fashion. Jamal and Torcher again headed off to drink from a nearby stream that splashed among some rocks, while Beatrice and I debated which of us should descend into the fishing village that we had seen at the eastern end of the peninsula. We wanted to buy something more interesting to eat than ship's biscuits, and Torcher had already made it clear that he needed to be fed too, by sitting with his head back and eyeing us with a distinctly forlorn expression.

Eventually we decided that Beatrice should go. She took the haversack and some of the coins that were in the pouch from the dragonological field kit and returned about two hours later carrying a loaf of bread and the haversack filled to the brim with goats' meat and chicken. While she was away, I had prepared a fire with dry sticks from a clump of nearby bushes. Torcher consumed his meal of goats' meat in a few moments and began playfully running in circles around Jamal, when what we really wanted him to do was light our campfire. We had been worried that Jamal would also want some goats' meat once he saw it, but he had shown no sign of hunger. Instead he got to his feet, walked over to the fire and started nosing around the pile of sticks.

"Look," said Beatrice. "What's Jamal up to?"

It was only when he sucked in a big lungful of air that we realised.

"Shumul, mai!" called Beatrice. *"Shumul, mai!"*

But it was too late. An enormous *WHOOSH* of flame burst out of Jamal's mouth and completely incinerated not only the campfire that I had built but also the bush behind it and all of the chicken.

"I think our meal's a little overdone," said Beatrice, holding up the chicken, which was now nothing more than a cinder.

"Maybe these biscuits aren't so bad, after all," I said.

After we had eaten, we set Torcher down with *Liber Draconis* and got him to breathe fire over it again. When the letters appeared on the cover, we once more began our search for the password we would need to ride the Dragon Express. Quickly we flicked through the section written in old-fashioned English, looking for anything that might be a password. About halfway through, we reached a part that had a clear title in both English and runes. It said *26th day of August 1566 — Cader Idris: Matters Practical*, but we had no time to read further, as just then Torcher gave a low growl. We had been so engrossed in the dragon diary that we had not heard the shouts coming up the valley towards us.

"Perhaps someone saw the fire!" exclaimed Beatrice.

As quickly as I could, I wrapped *Liber Draconis* in a piece of the flameproof cloak, since it was still red-hot. Then we hastily collected our belongings and in a trice were back on Jamal, who made a short run before taking off, then swooped up and over the still-smoking remains of the bush, where a very surprised group of villagers stood looking at us with wide-eyed amazement. As they had plainly seen us, there was nothing else to do but wave at them, wish them a hearty "Good day!" and hope that no one would believe their story of flying dragons and strange children who burned bushes and disappeared without so much as a by your leave.

That night, we made our way south across the middle

of Spain. We passed over more mountains, then low hills, before reaching a vast flat plain dotted with cattle and herds of horses. I was pleased to see that there really *were* little clusters of windmills here and there, just as I had expected from reading *Don Quixote* at school. Finally we reached the south coast, where Jamal landed among the dunes on a windy, deserted beach.

He was getting much better at landing, although we did get covered in a spray of sand as he touched down. It had been cold crossing Spain at night, but it was very warm during the day, so we rigged up one of the travelling capes as a sunshade.

I felt dirty and decided to go for a swim in the sea. Both Torcher and Jamal, who had never seen the sea that close before, were transfixed by my behaviour as I undressed and went down to the water wearing only my undertrousers. Clearly thinking that I must have gone mad, Jamal even tried to rescue me after I had dived in, wading up to his thighs in the surf and trying to pull me out by grabbing me gently between his huge jaws. Torcher, meanwhile, ran back and forth out of reach of the waves until Beatrice fetched him to help her light a fire she had built from driftwood. When I had finished bathing, we boiled some of our dried beans with a little dried meat and peppers. It was not the best meal I had ever tasted, but it was a decided relief to have a change from biscuits.

Not having got far with *Liber Draconis* the previous day, we were glad when Torcher blew a large jet of flame over it, so that the letters remained illuminated for longer. We soon found the section entitled *26th day of August 1566 – Cader Idris: Matters Practical* again.

On the page that followed, we found a picture of a large gem encircled by a long, thin dragon with its tail in its mouth.

"Isn't that the Talisman of Master Merlin?" said Beatrice. "Another of the twelve treasures of the S.A.S.D.?"

"Yes," I said excitedly. "And look! There seems to be a spell next to it, written out in runes. That must be the spell that gives you command over a dragon! I remember Dr. Drake telling us about it. We won't need the password if we can command dragons, will we?"

"Daniel," said Beatrice sternly, "we are not here to command dragons but to help conserve and protect them. Now, let's just carry on with what we're meant to be looking for, shall we?"

I groaned, but I knew that she was right.

We turned several more pages until we found a section that had illustrations of two different chalices on each page. Each chalice had a list of words written on it in runes and a short runic description underneath. We quickly translated the texts and found them to be a mixture of spells and recipes, with lists of ingredients. There was a spell for resisting heat, a recipe for feeding baby amphitheres, a method of making invisible ink from dragon scales — which I thought was funny in a book that contained writing that was itself usually invisible — and a list of uses for dragon dung. Finally, we came across a page that showed what looked like a flying carpet, with an illustration of a feather beside it and, opposite, a series of four pictures showing different dragons, each with a rider on its back: one flying over an elephant on a hill, the other over a ship on the sea, another over a castle and a fourth over a desert with camels. At the bottom of the page was a single long word and what looked like an empty picture frame.

"Do you think this could be it?" I asked. "A sequence of dragons with riders?"

"I'm not sure," said Beatrice. "Let's translate it."

The runes by the flying carpet were straightforward enough — they said *19th day of September — Avalon — Phoenix Feather Spell* — but the title above the images of the four dragons and the long word that we hoped might be the password were written in what looked like runes at first glance, but different runes from those we had learned with Dr. Drake. It was as if they were somehow backwards. We were stumped.

What would we do if we reached Uwassa and still didn't know the password?

✳

That night, we set off once more on Jamal and crossed the sea to reach Morocco. Here the land quickly became dry desert, and instead of heading directly inland, as Beatrice and I had expected, Jamal stayed near the coast, where the land was greener. We flew over a few towns and even some large cities, although the desert often came right up to the shore. Jamal always chose to land in the most deserted spots, so we did not get the opportunity to buy any more fresh meat, but we had enough food in our bags, and he always stopped near some kind of water source each morning. We did not see as many animals as we had done crossing Spain, although we did see herds of sheep and cultivated fields, and there were plenty of fishing boats out on the sea, which were visible by the lights at the top of their masts. We had seen no other dragons during our entire journey, but on our second night crossing North Africa, I was sure that

I saw a dragon far off in the distance just before dawn. I thought it was a wyvern, like Jamal, but it did not come near us, which was a shame. Had it been friendly, I would have certainly asked it about the strange runes that were still puzzling us.

During the long hours of our journey, I spent much time wondering what might be happening to our friends. Were Nia and Mademoiselle Gamay safe? Had Dr. Drake managed to find our parents? Had Panthéon survived his battle with the gargouilles?

"What are you thinking about?" asked Beatrice, when she noticed my worried expression. When I shared my fears, she gave me a reassuring squeeze.

"All we can do, Daniel, is concentrate on our mission and pray that everyone will be all right. Worrying won't get us anywhere. That's what Mother would say."

✳

The next day we made a very interesting discovery in *Liber Draconis*. We had continued to search through it, in case we found a glossary for the difficult runes, or in case there was some more information about the Dragon Express. About thirty pages after the spells section was another section in English. It was in much more modern English than the earlier passage, and it read as follows:

On Sickness

Sickness is an intriguing study. Dragons rarely fall ill; humans — as the science of humanology reveals — fall ill all too often. When I was young and on my travels, there was a time of dragon sickness. A dragon-hating king sent clever men far to find the means to rid his kingdom of dragons, and these men finally discovered a disease to afflict us, spreading it in the form of a terrible black powder. Only after many dragons had died was a cure found, mixed according to a special recipe in a chalice named after an ancient healer of dragons, and what was left of that deadly powder was sealed away in a cave hidden beneath a river on this, the Lost Isle of Dragons. Only once since that time has the cave's secret lock been broken, and a vial of that evil dust been removed. In whose hands it be, and for what ends, I never discovered, but fear that only ill can come of it.

Beneath the writing was a faint outline of a red chalice. On it was a single word, *Brimstone*, and beneath it, two lines, which read:

My first is in veins but not in blood,
My second is in squawk but not in hoot.

"This must be it!" I cried. "The recipe that Dr. Drake needs to cure the nagas. Perhaps Alexandra got hold of some of this black powder, and that's what is making them so ill!"

"Yes," agreed Beatrice. "But these two lines don't sound much like a recipe to me, more like the beginning of a riddle."

"There must be more," I said, rapidly turning the leaves, but all that followed were three blank pages in a row, and then one that read, *25th December 1820 – Snow – Ben Wyvis: Tracking and Taming Humans.*

"But this is all there is," said Beatrice.

"Unless the rest has been rubbed out," I replied.

"Or is still invisible," said Beatrice.

Then even the words that we *could* see began to fade.

"Anyway, it's not the password," she said. "And that's the really important thing at the moment."

"If only Panthéon could have told us what it was!" I said.

"Maybe he didn't know what it was himself," said Beatrice. "Or he would have told us, wouldn't he?"

Chapter XII
NGORONGORO

A wyvern's home is best understood as encompassing the whole range wherein it hunts; interlopers are seldom tolerated.
— Liber Draconis, 'Key Features of Different Dragons'

"Look!" I cried to Beatrice. "The pyramids! I've always wanted to see the pyramids."

It was several hours later and we were flying over the moonlit landscape of Egypt. When we had reached what I guessed from its size must be the mouth of the Nile, Jamal had turned south and begun to follow the river inland, obeying some deep instinct that was drawing him back to his true home. First we had passed over the Delta, where the river flows into many different channels before reaching the sea. In the dark, the thousands of tiny lights from the settlements along the banks of the river looked just like stars. Then we had reached the city of Cairo, spread out below us in the growing light of dawn. I had not expected to see the pyramids, but, to my delight, there they were, looking much smaller from this height than I had imagined.

We made camp in an oasis to the west of the pyramids. Our question about when Jamal might want to eat was now answered, for he finally went hunting — an excellent sign that he would be able to survive by himself in the wild. Once we had landed, he gave us a long look, as though to reassure us that he would soon return, then he flew off over the desert. He came back two hours later, when the day had grown very hot, looking exceedingly pleased with himself. After settling himself down, he coughed up a great fur ball that, on closer inspection, seemed to be the remains of a rather charred camel. Jamal may have been content, but Torcher certainly was not. Instead of sitting with Jamal, as was his usual habit, he took himself off to the very edge of the oasis, facing out into the desert.

"Do you think he's upset that Jamal didn't bring him any food?" I said.

"I expect so," said Beatrice.

Whatever the reason, when it was time to start our cooking fire and read some more of the dragon diary, Torcher kept running away. When we caught up with him, he stopped us from tickling him under the chin by holding his head firmly down against his neck.

I remonstrated with him, but it was no good.

"Why don't we try using Jamal?" suggested Beatrice. "Or do you think he'd incinerate the book, the way he did our chicken dinner?"

We decided that *Liber Draconis* was probably impervious to dragon fire, however strong, but unfortunately, Jamal was no help at all. No matter how much we coaxed him or tickled him under the chin, he simply would not breathe fire over the book.

"I could start a fire myself, if Torcher hadn't stolen my fire-lighting materials," I said to him.

"But you still *can* start it yourself," said Beatrice, jumping up. "Isn't there a magnifying glass in that field kit? You could try using that to magnify the sun's rays."

"Good idea," I said. "But it's not going to help us with *Liber Draconis*. We need dragon fire for that. At this rate, we'll have to fly Jamal all the way to India!"

Nevertheless, I went to look for the magnifying glass. When I tipped out the contents of the haversack, the small piece of mirror from the field kit also fell out beside it.

With a sudden flash of understanding, I remembered the empty picture frame that had been next to the strange runes in *Liber Draconis*. It wasn't a picture frame at all — it was a mirror!

I wasn't able to test out the theory that had formed in my mind until the following day, when Torcher finally stopped sulking and breathed fire for us again. Once I had found the spot in the dragon diary with the strange runes, I held the mirror up to the page.

"Look, Bea," I said. "It's not a special kind of rune that we can't read — it's just mirror writing!"

And sure enough, now we could translate the runes. They said, *Password for the Dragon Express:* *HONORIFIC-ABILITUDINI-TATIBUS.*

After our first stop in Egypt, it took us a further two nights of flying up the river to reach Lake Victoria. There, we spent a few uncomfortable hours camped among clouds of buzzing insects near to its banks — but not too near, for fear of crocodiles. Jamal, of course, was not bothered by either of these things, but Torcher seemed very unsettled and spent his time snapping at anything in sight. So it was a relief when Jamal got up shortly after noon and nudged us both to let us know that he was eager to be off.

Although it was still daylight, the land below was

virtually uninhabited, so we stopped worrying about being spotted. Jamal flew with an urgency that I had not seen in him before, and I wondered if he sensed that he was nearing home. Soon he was flying so swiftly that we had crossed both Lake Victoria and the forest on the other side, and had finally reached the wide, grassy plains of the Serengeti.

"There!" cried Beatrice, pointing at something on the ground. "Aren't they giraffes?"

I looked down and saw that Beatrice was right. There were many other animals, too: wildebeest, zebras and elephants. Jamal would have good hunting here, of that I was sure. He flew quickly towards a huge crater in the landscape, circled it three times, then swooped in over the edge. As he flew lower, I could see that there was a herd of zebras feeding not very far away from an elephant.

Jamal hovered, his wing beats keeping him almost motionless in the air as he surveyed this new territory. There was a forest that covered the steep sides of the crater and then grassland that finally gave way to wide salt flats surrounding a lake coloured pink with millions of wading flamingos. In the sunlight, I could see our small shadows dancing on the crater's grassy floor. Jamal made a deep rumbling noise and looked

"There!" cried Beatrice, pointing at something on the ground.
"Aren't they giraffes?"

back at us over his shoulder. He was home.

As we watched, a pride of lions emerged from the long grass. Two lionesses crouched low and ran wide to get behind a herd of zebras, which seemed oblivious to the fact that they were being stalked.

"Look out!" shouted Beatrice. "Hey!"

"What do you mean, 'look out'?" I said. "The zebras can't hear you and anyway, the lions do have to eat, you know."

Beatrice ignored me. Torcher was now looking down at the scene below us as well.

The lionesses made their move, streaking towards the zebras while the rest of the pride charged in from the other direction. The panicked herd scattered in a terrific muddle, and in the resulting confusion, the two lionesses closed in on a zebra foal that had lost its mother and was trying its best to run away.

Beatrice gasped. So did I, but for a completely different reason: I had spotted a dark but familiar shadow on the ground, moving quickly towards our own.

The lions stopped their pursuit of the zebra foal, looked upwards and tore away across the grassland. The zebras, which had gathered together again, stampeded away with the foal cantering along behind them. The elephant, which had been seemingly indifferent to the whole business up to now, trumpeted wildly and bolted, trampling trees in its path and fleeing towards the salt flats, where it was soon wading up to its knees.

"Beatrice," I said in a small voice, "it's another wyvern."

We turned to look. It certainly was a wyvern. And what a wyvern! It was huge, almost the size of a small house, ten or fifteen times the size of Jamal at least, and it was bearing straight down on us at terrific speed. Now we were the ones who were being hunted. The wyvern's talons alone seemed to be a foot long, and when it let out an angry roar, the whole crater shook with the sound. In reply, Torcher let out a frightened mew, and Jamal, who had only just noticed the threat, dived out of the sky. The territory he had chosen was, apparently, already occupied. He streaked downwards towards some trees by the edge of the lake, and I had a horrible feeling that I knew what he was going to do.

"No, Jamal!" I cried. "*Gerupthar! GERUPTHAR! ALGRAI!*"

"*Mai, Shumul, mai!*" shouted Beatrice as the wyvern neared ground level. "We can't land here! Lions! There are lions here!"

But Jamal did not understand. He briefly landed and,

without waiting for us to dismount, gently tipped us off onto the ground, then flew quickly away with the other wyvern in hot pursuit.

"Are you all right?" asked Beatrice after she had got to her feet, dusting herself off and collecting a disgruntled-looking Torcher.

"Yes," I said. I looked around, half-expecting the lionesses to burst out of the undergrowth at any moment. Then I had an idea.

"The lake!" I gasped. "We might be safer there!"

Beatrice nodded. The lake was three hundred yards away at least, but the salt flats did not seem far. I wondered if the lions would follow us onto them. We began to run.

Out on the salt flats, we did not sink into the earth as the elephant had, but it was hard going. Torcher squirmed and clung to Beatrice's shoulders, looking down anxiously. We were striding, rather than running, towards the lake now. The going became more and more difficult. Suddenly, a lioness appeared to one side of us, quickly followed by a second lioness. They looked across at us, sniffed the air, then paused.

"Perhaps Torcher's smell is confusing her," I said.

The lionesses each gingerly put out a paw. They

glanced towards the trees, then suddenly they both turned tail and vanished!

"Jamal?" Beatrice cried hopefully.

But it was not Jamal who came out from among the trees. It was the other wyvern, a glossy giant that stood watching us intently. The elephant, far away now, reached the far edge of the grassland and disappeared into the steep forest along the sides of the crater.

The wyvern made no move towards the salt flats. Instead, it stretched out its wings, and then, to our great surprise, it spoke.

"Prrrraisich hoyarrrri!" Its deep voice boomed across the flats.

Beatrice and I gasped.

"Praisich boyar!" I shouted back, at which the wyvern came forwards until it was towering over us. "Do you speak English?" I asked.

"I speak many languages," the wyvern answered, "though not all of them as well as I would like."

"We are seeking a wyvern named Uwassa," I continued nervously.

"You know my name, then, children," replied the wyvern. "What is the name of the young dragon who brought you here?"

"Jamal," I said.

"A handsome name," said Uwassa.

"Is he all right?" cried Beatrice.

"He is well," said the wyvern. "I merely discouraged him from taking an interest in my hunting ground — that is all."

He made a gesture with his wing to a place where, with great relief, I could make out Jamal perched high up on the rim of the crater, about half a mile away. He was looking back at us.

"I understand he has returned to live in the wild, where he belongs. That is as it should be," said the huge dragon, bending his head to look at us more closely.

"We will miss him," said Beatrice, tearfully, and almost as if he could hear us, Jamal put his head back and let out a mighty roar before spreading his wings and disappearing over the edge of the crater. At this point, Torcher let out a plaintive squeak and clung to Beatrice even more. Uwassa lowered his great head further and whispered something to the little dragon, who immediately relaxed.

"You have brought this dragon chick far from home," said Uwassa.

"We had to escape," said Beatrice. "We are on a

mission for the Society of Dragons, and we need to use the Dragon Express."

"Indeed?" said Uwassa.

"You see, we have a book," I continued nervously. "It is called *Liber Draconis*. And we have a chalice too, which was named after Saint Petroc, and—"

"And it is very important that we deliver them to a place called Jaisalmer in India as soon as possible," interrupted Beatrice. "The dragons there are dying from a terrible sickness."

"I see," said Uwassa.

"And the Dragon Express is supposed to take us there," I explained.

"We have a password," Beatrice added hopefully.

"Do you, indeed?" said Uwassa. "Then you'd better tell me it."

"Let's say it together," whispered Beatrice to me. *"Honorific-abilitudini-tatibus!"* we cried.

The great sandy-coloured dragon looked impressed.

"Show me this book you are carrying."

I took *Liber Draconis* out and laid it on the ground. Uwassa sniffed it.

"The writing appears only when a dragon breathes fire on it," I said.

"Then stand back," said Uwassa. He blew out a gust of flame over the book. The letters of the title, *Liber Draconis*, lit up as before, although there was a difference. This time they were blue.

Uwassa turned the pages with his claw.

"I have not looked at many books before," he said. "But this one is interesting. There are pictures of elephants, camels, assegais. African things. You did not mention that it was written by a wyvern."

We had never seen any wyverns or assegais in the book. We leaned over it. The book looked so different that at first I thought it couldn't be the same one. But Uwassa was right. It *did* have pictures of wyverns in it now, and the maps showed trade routes and places in Africa.

"How...?" I asked.

"I don't know," said Beatrice.

Quickly she flicked through to the page that had been titled "On Sickness." This time, the first page was blank, but on the second page there was another picture of a chalice, only blue, and some blue writing that read: *Tears of Isis*.

Beneath the chalice were another two lines of what now definitely appeared to be a riddle. They read,

My third is in wise but not in fool,
My fourth is in apple but not in fruit.

There was nothing else, but Beatrice looked at me excitedly. I knew why.

"Now I understand!" she exclaimed.

"Understand what?" said Uwassa.

"Something amazing," said Beatrice. "This book has a secret that we have only just discovered. The fire of different species of dragon makes it show different things!"

Uwassa seemed unimpressed. "Let us return to the matter at hand," he said. "You have told me the password for the Dragon Express, and so I will take you onwards. I will take you as far as Arabia, to a place known to humans as Harat Kishb. There you must find a second dragon to complete your journey. She has three names: Faki, Kifa and Kafi. You will find her in a lava cave on an extinct volcano. Let us go."

"Why has she got three names?" said Beatrice.

"Because she has three heads, of course," said Uwassa. "She is a hydra, and each of her heads has a different name. Now, let us go."

"But what about Jamal?" I asked.

Then I suddenly realised that Jamal really had gone

for good — his last roar had been his roar good-bye. Torcher had understood. I felt a lump in my throat. I had always known that we were going to return Jamal to the wild — it was where he belonged. But we had travelled so far with him and he had taken such good care of us that it made me very sad to think that we might never see him again. I guessed that Beatrice was feeling the same. She reached out and held my hand.

"Jamal has seen that you are safe," said Uwassa. "He has returned to a place where he can be happy. Maybe you will pass this way again one day. Then, you might see him once more."

"But it's such a long way," I said.

"It may be a long way to your home," said Uwassa, "but at least it is not so far to Harat Kishb, for I am a very fast flier. So, climb on, my young adventurers, and let's be on our way."

Chapter XIII
THE DRAGON EXPRESS

The hydra is one of the few dragons to love discussion and debate;
it rarely agrees even with itself.

— Liber Draconis, 'Key Features of Different Dragons'

Uwassa was as good as his word, but it still took us two days to reach Harat Kishb. Riding on him was much more comfortable than on Jamal, for he was an experienced flier and the spines along his back were so big that they provided excellent back rests. He also flew higher than Jamal, out of sight of anyone below. We did not therefore bother about flying only at night, and we used our goggles to shield our eyes from the bright sun. Uwassa flew so quickly that it sometimes felt as if we were flying through a gale as the air rushed past us. Once he was fully airborne, he soon found a stream of air that allowed him to make only occasional movements of his wings to keep himself aloft and moving swiftly.

At first Uwassa had taken us north again, retracing

much of our journey with Jamal up the Nile. Beneath us, savanna turned to jungle turned to mountain turned to desert, before we landed and made camp next to an ancient ruined temple with four broken statues of gigantic, seated pharaohs around a darkened, sealed doorway.

That night Uwassa proved to be a thoughtful companion. After setting us down, he disappeared for about half an hour and returned bearing a basket containing dates, bread and some fresh meat, although from where we did not enquire. We had not found any wood for a fire, but he answered this need too by boiling the meat himself in our cooking pot with occasional puffs of flame. This task done, he asked us to let him look at *Liber Draconis*. After breathing fire over it, he spent several hours sitting beside Torcher, poring over the book.

By dawn we were moving again. We passed over a strip of sea dotted with boats that was bordered on each side by bright desert. Here, Uwassa started to descend, and below us, the landscape changed to one made up of dark-looking hills, where the ground appeared like a twisted, gnarled lava field covered with small rocks.

"We are arriving in the empty quarter of Arabia," said Uwassa. "Harat Kishb lies beneath us."

✳

We landed on a ledge halfway up the side of a dark red mountain that smelled of dry sulphur, and from there, Beatrice and I looked out on one of the strangest, most desolate landscapes I have ever seen. Torcher put out a foot and touched one of the black rocks with his claws, then looked up at Uwassa as though he wanted to climb up on his back again and leave immediately.

"I wish you luck in your quest," said Uwassa. "You will find the next dragon of the Dragon Express — Faki-Kifa-Kafi — in a cave to the north."

"Can't you introduce us?" I asked.

"There is no need," replied Uwassa, "and I would rather not. The hydra might have seen us coming. Kafi might not mind, but Faki and Kifa will not like me entering their territory without permission. And is it not usual for dragonologists to introduce *themselves* to dragons? If you have been entrusted with delivering ancient and precious treasures, then surely you have learned that?"

Uwassa bowed his head down towards Torcher, and they touched noses.

"Make sure you keep this young one safe," he said. "And now, farewell!" Then Uwassa launched himself into the air and was soon gone.

...Uwassa launched himself into the air and was soon gone.

"Well, at least there aren't any lions here," I said as we set off in the direction that Uwassa had indicated.

"But Faki-Kifa-Kafi sounds complicated," said Beatrice. "I don't think we were ever taught about dealing with hydras, were we?"

Our progress quickly became a scramble. The side of the mountain was very steep in places and covered with loose rock, so we had to be careful where we put our weight. As we climbed, the wind grew stronger. Torcher, who was now feeling quite at home, gambolled on ahead. At one stage, he found a black snake that he gobbled down with delight. It occurred to me that he had just caught his very first meal.

"I don't like this at all!" shouted Beatrice. "It's rocky and horrible and I've just stubbed my toe!"

"I don't like it either!" I shouted. "But we don't have much of a choice. Let's just hope that we aren't too far from that cave and that Faki-Kifa-Kafi is as friendly as Uwassa."

"At least Torcher seems to be enjoying himself," said Beatrice.

But at that moment, Torcher, who was only about fifteen yards ahead of us up the slope, suddenly vanished. We ran up the slope after him and found a gaping black hole that disappeared almost vertically into the side of the mountain.

"Torcher!" cried Beatrice. "Come back!"

But there was no sign at all of the dragon chick.

"Quick!" said Beatrice. "We've got to go down into that cave and find him!"

Just over the lip of the hole, a series of boulders jutting from the walls formed a staircase down into the depths. They were so regular in shape that I guessed they must have been made by humans in some long-forgotten era when the cave had been inhabited.

We climbed down into the darkness and soon found ourselves on a solid floor. It was cooler in the cave, and the wind didn't bother us, although it still howled mournfully overhead. Our eyes adjusted to the gloom, and we could see that the cave went further back, going downwards at a slight angle towards a distant, polished black wall that I could only just make out. There was no sign of Torcher anywhere, but there were some vague rustling sounds that I could not identify coming from the rear of the cave. There was also a slightly sour smell and another sulphurous odour that I knew to be a clear indication of the presence of dragons.

"Torcher!" I hissed.

Somewhere in the darkness, Torcher hiccupped. Then he let out a jet of flame. The roof of the cave, lit up by Torcher's brief fire, proved to be a mass of bats, which took wing at once, squeaking and flapping. I felt them rushing past my ear, and Beatrice screamed as one nearly became tangled in her hair. I pulled her to the floor as the bats wheeled past us, up out of the cave and into the air.

Torcher let out several more gobbits of flame, and I could see that he was leaping up in the air, trying to catch the bats as they skimmed above him. As they thinned out, I was amazed to see the back wall of the cave rise up and unfurl to reveal two black wings, while six yellow eyes suddenly opened wide and trained themselves on the dragon chick.

In two steps, the dragon — which had three heads on three grey, scaly necks and a long, spiked tail — was upon him. It was the hydra, and although it was nowhere near as big as Uwassa, it was certainly big enough. Torcher roared at the hydra, glancing from head to head as he did so. One of the heads sniffed inquisitively towards him, while another looked back at what I realised was a huge pile of treasure — gold and gems, with bones scattered all around.

I stood up and cried, "Faki-Kifa-Kafi!"

All three heads jerked as one towards me.

"Praisich boyar," I said.

"Fiddlesticks!" said the third head.

Torcher roared again.

Then the three heads turned back towards the dragon chick and roared in unison, ten times louder than Torcher, so that the whole cave shook with the savage harmony of their different voices.

Torcher bared his teeth, hiccupped, then spat out another jet of flame. It lapped uselessly around the hydra's right knee.

"A spirited little fellow, isn't he?" said the first head.

"Let's eat him," said the third.

"We must drive them all away before they steal our treasure," said the other.

"At least she's only got three heads," I whispered to Beatrice. "Imagine if she had ten!"

"To whom do we have the pleasure of speaking?" continued the first head.

"Or displeasure," said the third.

"My name is Daniel, and this is my sister, Beatrice," I said.

"And this is Torcher," said Beatrice, pointing to our

"To whom do we have the pleasure of speaking?"

charge, who had now run round to hide behind her legs.

"Bat Scarer might be a better name," said the second head.

"Or Cinder. That might be even better," said the third, "for that is what he will become if he is not extremely careful."

Torcher bristled.

"Excuse me," I said, "but which one of you is which?"

"Do not tell them," said the second head to the third.

"I won't," said the third.

"I will tell them then," said the first. "My name is Kafi. This is Faki," she continued, pointing to the third head. "And this is Kifa. But to what do we owe the pleasure? Humans so rarely visit us these days."

"We require the services of the Dragon Express," said Beatrice. "We must travel to a place called Jaisalmer in India."

"We're on an important mission," I added.

"What mission?" asked Faki.

"We have treasures that we must deliver," I said, pointing to our small bag. "A chalice and a book."

"You must tell us the password then," said Kafi.

"I bet they don't know it," said Faki.

"Honorific-abilitudini-tatibus!" we cried together.

Faki looked disappointed. "So you do know it," she said. "Tell us more about the treasures."

"Are you sure they don't belong to us?" added Kifa.

"Don't mind them," said Kafi. "We will take you to Jaisalmer, in Rajasthan. There is a palace there inside a walled city. Is that your destination?"

"Yes," we answered.

"I expect it's full of treasure," said Kifa.

"I think we should know about these treasures," interrupted Faki, "if we have to carry them all the way to India."

So we explained all that we knew about Saint Petroc's Chalice and *Liber Draconis*.

"Shall we try breathing fire over this book?" said Kafi.

"Yes!" chorused the other two.

We followed Faki-Kifa-Kafi outside, and Beatrice held Torcher while I placed *Liber Draconis* on the ground. The hydra banged its three heads together, making a fearful noise.

"Why are you doing that?" I asked.

"To get the sparks going, of course," said Faki.

Suddenly, three jets of flame erupted from Faki-Kifa-Kafi's three mouths. They were red, yellow and green, and they completely bathed *Liber Draconis* in fire. The words on the cover, however, did not light up, and when we looked inside, the pages remained completely blank.

"Well, I never," said Beatrice. "A hydra can't be one of the dragon species used to make the book's contents visible."

"Typical!" said Faki.

"They never ask us to do anything," said Kifa.

"Except to be part of the Dragon Express," said Kafi.

✳

The flight on Faki-Kifa-Kafi proved to be the most comfortable of all our dragon rides, for the hydra's spines were very small and we both had a neck to sit astride. But when we first stepped from the cave, Torcher refused to get on at all. Beatrice and I made it clear that we were going to get on whether he liked it or not — by strapping the flameproof cloaks onto two of the hydra's necks, for padding — whereupon Torcher relented and climbed up onto the first neck.

"Don't worry, little dragon," said Kafi. "I won't let you fall."

The journey took three days and three nights, much of it over dry, dusty terrain, with hardly any sign of humans at all. The hydra, which kept up an almost constant bickering with itself, seemed to have amazing stamina and allowed us only the briefest of stops during each night.

On the second night, after a long debate about which head was the hungriest, Faki-Kifa-Kafi left us to catch some food. She returned with some gazelle meat, which she shared with Torcher and then argued with herself about incessantly — until Beatrice had had enough.

"Will you just be quiet and let us get some sleep?" she said.

The three heads fell to mumbling, but other than that they did not disturb us for the rest of that night.

Chapter XIV
JAISALMER

*Maharawal (Hindi): great (maha) king (rawal). A title most
commonly used by the rulers of Jaisalmer and Dungarpur.
Alternatives: maharajah, maharawat, maharana, maharao.*
— Liber Draconis, 'Glossary'

Faki-Kifa-Kafi left us in a desert about a mile from
the gates of a hilltop town that had outgrown its
original walls and now spread out into the valley, right
up to the shore of a small lake dotted with stone pavilions.

"Jaisalmer at last!" I said, recognising it from the
many pictures Dr. Drake had shown us.

It felt very strange to be staring at the town where
our parents had spent so much time and from which
we'd received so many letters. I had to stifle an urge to
run up to the town and immediately start enquiring
about our parents or Dr. Drake. We needed to be careful.
We had Torcher to think of, and we'd come so far to get
here that we didn't want to make any mistakes now.

Near the entrance to the town, along the road, there seemed to be a number of stalls selling local produce. Beatrice and I agreed that she would wait with Torcher while I went to try and find something to hide him in. Although the first few stalls sold mainly food — which made my mouth water — I soon came to one selling woven baskets of the type used by Indian snake charmers. I managed to buy one that looked about the right size by holding out a few coins, and returned with it to Beatrice.

Torcher, having got used to his freedom, wasn't at all pleased at being placed in a basket. He flapped his wings and kicked mercilessly whenever we tried to lift him in. Then Beatrice placed a couple of gems and *Liber Draconis* inside. Seeing the book — or perhaps the huge glowing gem in the cover — at the bottom of the basket, Torcher climbed in willingly and curled up with the book between his talons. There was room for the chalice too, so we discarded our old bag and each grabbed hold of one of the basket's handles, then set off up the hill. We made our way along the main street and into a large open space, then up some wide steps to the gate of the walled part of the town. Above us, rising majestically from behind the walls, was a huge building with flags on it — I guessed that it was the Maharawal's Palace.

There were guards at the gate. They were carrying rifles and were dressed in starched white uniforms and helmets with plumes. They watched as we approached.

I realised that we must stand out like two sore thumbs — an English boy and girl carrying a large wicker basket up to the gates of an Indian town.

"Don't you think we look rather conspicuous?" I said.

"Just keep walking," Beatrice whispered irritably. "And try to look as if you do this every day."

One of the guards, who was wearing a cap and carrying a short cane, seemed to be the chief guard. He said something to us as we drew nearer to the gate, but we could not understand him.

"We are English," said Beatrice. "Do you speak English?"

But the guards just looked at us blankly.

Beatrice tried another tack.

"We are here to see the Maharawal of Jaisalmer," she said. "Please inform him that the Cooks' children have arrived and that we would like to be escorted to see him at once."

The chief guard did not reply. Instead he pointed at the basket and made a gesture to suggest that we should lift up the lid so that he could look inside.

"Impossible," said Beatrice, shaking her head. "Very sick animal inside. Very sick."

She mimed being sick and pointed to the basket.

The chief guard did not seem amused. He shouted to one of his men, who took the basket containing Torcher from us and put it on the ground. He lifted the lid up, and Torcher's head came snaking out of the top. The guard's eyes grew wide, and there was a brief pause before all the guards started shouting at once.

"Now we're in for it," I said.

The chief pushed the lid roughly back down and shouted something to the others, who surrounded us. Then they marched us in through the gates and up to the palace. Another guard carried the wicker basket, but when it started to roar and shake, he quickly put it down again.

"Do you think they're going to lock us up?" I asked.

"Worse," said Beatrice. "Look!"

The guards were all aiming their rifles at the basket.

Suddenly there was a shout from the palace gates. A regal-looking boy, who appeared to be only a few years older than we were, dressed in a short black jacket, a long white shirt and long white trousers, was coming towards us. The guards immediately shouldered their rifles and bowed to him.

The boy smiled.

"Are you English?" he said.

"Yes," Beatrice. "We are the son and daughter of Mr. and Mrs. Cook."

"You mean to say that you are Daniel and Beatrice?" he said with a gasp.

"Yes, we are," I replied. "Has anyone heard any news of our parents?"

The boy looked at the ground, as though he didn't know what to say.

"I'm sorry to say that we haven't heard anything since they left to return to England. My uncle, the Maharawal, is searching for signs of them as we speak, and also for their missing colleague Noah Hayes, who has not returned from his trip into the Thar Desert. My uncle says that he will not give up the search until they are all found."

"What about Dr. Drake?" asked Beatrice.

"Dr. Drake came to Jaisalmer about two weeks ago, but he has left too," said the boy. "But what are *you* doing here? How on earth did you get here?"

"Er, well, we rode," I said, not sure if we should keep the Dragon Express a secret.

"To Jaisalmer? But how—?" said the boy. "Forgive me. I am forgetting my manners. Allow me to introduce myself. I am Ranjit Singh, Prince of Jaisalmer. I am very pleased to meet you, even if you do come at a very sad time. Indeed, I almost feel that I know you already — I have heard so much about you."

"We are very pleased to meet you, too," said Beatrice.

"Now let us go inside. I am sure you will be in need of refreshments after such a long trip."

Beatrice and I picked up the basket and followed the prince into the palace through a pair of carved gates.

"I must apologise for the guards," said Prince Ranjit. "But you can't really blame them for their attitude towards you."

"Why is that?" said Beatrice. "Don't they speak English? I thought everyone in India spoke English."

"Then please accept my apologies for telling you that you know little about my country," said Prince Ranjit. "Here in Jaisalmer, which can be reached only by — er — camel, of course, we are famed for our remoteness."

By now we had arrived at a series of large rooms. Although the decor was, as far as I was concerned, strange and exotic, I guessed that they must be Prince Ranjit's rooms, for there were pictures of soldiers and cannons, a map of Europe, a map of India, four different cricket bats, a leather football and a set of rather battered-looking three-quarter-sized golf clubs. There were also two small pictures, one of a naga and the other of a European dragon. I wondered if they had been presents from my parents.

"Now," the prince said, stopping by a large mirror, "I will show you why the guards were reluctant to let you in through the city gate. They thought you must be beggars!" He laughed. "Just look at yourselves!"

Two of the dirtiest children we had ever seen looked back at us from the ornate mirror. It's true that I had noticed Beatrice was getting a bit grubby, but it was only now that I appreciated the full effect. I hadn't had a bath since I had been for a swim in the ocean, and the travel-worn clothes that we had hastily put on when we left Castle Drake were tatty and, I dare say, pretty smelly.

"And so," said Prince Ranjit, "you must borrow some clothes and have a bath."

"Thank you," I said. "But we've got to find Dr. Drake as soon as possible."

"As you wish," said Prince Ranjit. "But you must at least allow me to feed you. What is in the basket, by the way? It seems to be moving."

Beatrice and I looked at each other. Feeling conspiratorial, I pointed my finger down to the ground. Prince Ranjit did the same.

"When a dragon flies...?" he said.

"He seeks it with his eyes!" I said.

"When a dragon roars...?"

"He holds it in his claws!" concluded Beatrice.

"Ah, yes, I remember," said Prince Ranjit. "The password of the Secret and Ancient Society of Dragonologists itself. I am so pleased to meet more fellow practitioners! So you are dragonologists just like your parents?"

"Well, apprentice ones," I answered.

"When did our parents disappear?" asked Beatrice. "Dr. Drake seemed to think that they had joined a ship well over a month ago."

"This is what we thought, too. We waved them good-bye, and they set out for Bombay, meaning to take a ship to London. But they never arrived in Bombay and never took that ship. It is very strange."

"Well, they aren't the only ones who have vanished," I said.

"What?" said Prince Ranjit.

"Other dragonologists have been disappearing, too.

It looks like they've been kidnapped."

"Kidnapped? But by whom?"

"Dr. Drake suspects a Russian dragonologist named Alexandra Gorynytchka is behind it all," said Beatrice. "We think so too."

"And why are you here?" asked Prince Ranjit.

"We have been sent on a mission to bring Dr. Drake two of the treasures of the Secret and Ancient Society of Dragonologists," I explained. "There is a book called *Liber Draconis* and a magical chalice that was named after Saint Petroc, the great dragon healer. We were told to bring them by the British Society of Dragons itself. The book contains a recipe for a cure that might help the nagas."

Prince Ranjit blanched.

"I am afraid it may be too late for the nagas."

"What do you mean?" I said. "You can't mean that *all* the nagas have died, surely?"

"I believe so," said Prince Ranjit.

I was horrified. Beatrice had gone pale.

"Do you know where Dr. Drake went when he left?" I asked.

"He went to China," said Prince Ranjit. "To a secret place called Hong Wei, to visit the monks in a temple there — they have been working on a cure for the dragon sickness. Perhaps he hopes to learn where your parents are being held. And perhaps he hopes that there may still be time to save some of the *lung*. You know that they've been affected too?"

I nodded.

"Then Daniel and I must travel to Hong Wei without delay," said Beatrice.

"Of course," said Prince Ranjit. "We shall go and find my uncle, the Maharawal. He will be able to help you travel onwards to China. Right now he is out in the desert looking for any clues that might help him understand what happened to your parents. He goes out every day, but all he finds is dead nagas. And now, my dragonological friends, you simply must answer my original question. What have you got in that basket? It is wobbling about most oddly."

"The basket?" I said. "You know, I think you're going to like this, Prince Ranjit."

With that, I lifted the lid and whistled. Then, bit by bit, like a snake-charmer's cobra, though looking far more comical, came Torcher's inquisitive head.

Prince Ranjit clapped his hands in delight.

"Oh, it's a European dragon! A European dragon!" he

said. "I have always wanted to see one! What is his name? It is a 'he', isn't it?"

"He's called Torcher," Beatrice said, laughing.

At that, Torcher hopped right out of the basket and allowed Prince Ranjit to pat him on the head.

"Just don't tickle him under the chin," I said with a laugh, "whatever you do."

Beatrice and I wanted to find the Maharawal at once, but Prince Ranjit insisted that we bathe, eat, drink and change our clothes first. His uncle was not due to return to the city until later that afternoon and could at that moment be almost anywhere within a day's ride of Jaisalmer.

When we were ready and looking more like Indian princelings than ordinary English schoolchildren, we took Torcher with us — along with a haversack containing the treasures and a hamper full of food and drink — and set out for the royal camel stables. There, Prince Ranjit picked out a camel for each of us. He showed us how to mount the animal and ride it, and once the hamper and Torcher's basket had been fastened on, we all set off at a brisk trot. I rode on the camel with Torcher, while Beatrice shouldered the haversack containing the

treasures, and soon we were loping along at a reasonably fast pace as we made our way into the desert.

Along the way, there wasn't much to see apart from sand dunes, but I decided to lift the top of Torcher's basket so that he could have a look around, too. This proved to be a big mistake. As soon as the dragon chick poked his head out of the rucksack, my camel, sensing that something was amiss, turned its head to look at Torcher. And that's just when Torcher got a case of the hiccups. He hiccupped once or twice, then shot out a jet of flame. The camel's eyes went wild, and then he bolted!

Soon Beatrice and Prince Ranjit were far behind me. And no matter what I did, the camel refused to stop.

We raced on and on for nearly half a mile. Then the camel suddenly stopped dead in its tracks. Something had obviously spooked it. Quickly I jumped down, anxious in case it took off again. Torcher, seeing me on the ground, climbed out of the basket and hopped down, too.

While Beatrice and Prince Ranjit were catching up with me, I picked Torcher up in my arms and looked around to see what might have frightened the camel. What I saw amazed me: curled around the stump of a dead tree, its eyes closed tight, was a creature with a human-like head and a snake's body. Brown spittle was coming from its mouth, and now that I stopped to notice, I could see several vultures wheeling in the sky above it. It was a naga! I did not know whether it was alive or dead, and so I approached it very carefully.

Suddenly, just as I got really close to it, the naga's eyes opened wide and it uttered a single, urgent word.

"Arrrrptuh!"

"Stop!" cried Prince Ranjit urgently as he drew alongside me.

"What?" I said.

"Stop! It is saying 'stop'! It is very sick," said Prince Ranjit.

All at once, I understood. I backed away and

shuddered. To think what I had been about to do! I was
carrying Torcher into the presence of a sick dragon!

"I am amazed to find a naga still alive," said Prince
Ranjit, "and I don't know how it has got here, so close to
the town, unless someone has brought it here deliberately."

A gun clicked behind us.

"No one brought it here, mate," said a sneering
cockney voice that sounded terribly familiar. "It came
all on its own. I think it was trying to drag itself to
Jaisalmer to warn the Maharawal about *me*."

We turned round. To my astonishment, standing in
front of us in a dusty black jacket was exactly the same

man who had been the ringleader of the fake policemen back at Castle Drake!

Next to him was a dark-skinned man in a slouch hat. He bore such a strong resemblance to Nia that I guessed it had to be Noah Hayes. His face was drawn and lifeless, and he was pointing a gun directly at us.

"What is wrong with Mr. Hayes?" exclaimed Prince Ranjit. "You have hypnotised him, haven't you?"

The man with yellow teeth spat.

"Nice and docile, isn't he, Your Royal Highness?"

Beatrice looked horrified.

"What have you done with Mademoiselle Gamay and Nia?" she cried.

"Well, little missy, I took your friends to see a nice Russian lady I know. But it's you she really wants to see. You may have got away from me in England, but it won't happen this time — I can promise you that. You can call me Shadwell, by the way."

Slowly Shadwell undid his jacket pocket. I couldn't believe my eyes when the dwarf dragon Flitz, who had given us so much trouble on our previous adventure with Dr. Drake, climbed out of his pocket and sat on Shadwell's shoulder, eyeing us wickedly. With a furious roar, Torcher leaped out of my arms to confront him.

Shadwell grinned.

Flitz flew off Shadwell's shoulder and began tugging at the haversack of treasures, which Beatrice was clutching tightly. Torcher roared again, angrily.

"I'd control that chick if I were you," said Shadwell, pointing his gun at me.

I had no choice but to obey. I picked up Torcher, who continued growling and squirming furiously as Flitz flew around Beatrice, tugging at the haversack until she was forced to drop it.

"Now, look here," said Prince Ranjit. "My uncle is the king around here, and his army will hunt you down if anything at all happens to me or to any of my—"

"Shut up," said Shadwell simply, cutting him off. "Now, let's see what we have here."

He opened the top of the haversack and emptied out the contents.

"An old book and a magic chalice," he exclaimed. "Didn't steal them, did you?"

"No, we did not!" said Beatrice. "They're, er, family heirlooms."

"Tommyrot!" said Shadwell, snapping his fingers.

Shadwell opened the book with his toe. He frowned. "Nothing inside, eh? A blank book," he said. "Best kind, if you ask me. I never was much of a reader. But she'll like to see it, all the same. If she doesn't want it, I get to sell it, see?"

He turned to the chalice. "This, on the other hand, she is going to love. Isn't she, Noah?"

Noah didn't say anything.

He turned to us. "Poor old Noah doesn't say much, does he?" He laughed.

"You beast!" said Beatrice.

"No need to be impolite," said Shadwell. "Now, it's time we got a move on. You two are coming with me. We can leave His Royal Highness here to walk back to Jaisalmer."

"Where are you going to take us?" said Beatrice.

"You'll see," said Shadwell.

He took out a dragon whistle and blew it.

After a few minutes, two enormous, fierce-looking, black European dragons appeared in the sky and flew down. They were nearly the size of Uwassa and would certainly have dwarfed Idraigir. At the front, each one had a driver, or dragon mahout, seated on a high-crested saddle, wrapped in a fur-lined leather suit and wearing goggles and a tight cap. Like jockeys, both were small men, and each held a short, hooked iron rod — known among elephant mahouts as an ankus — in one hand and a long chain bridle attached to the dragon's mouth in the other. Along the beasts' backs were squat towers with iron shutters that looked like the howdahs once used on fighting elephants. Whether the dragons had been tamed by some combination of hypnosis, charm or dire threat I had no idea, but each came silently to earth and waited, motionless, while the mahouts scrambled along their backs to throw rope ladders to the ground. As the nearest ladder fell, I smelled a pungent aroma that I recognised as spearmint. Meanwhile, the dragons waited meekly, their eyes dull and lifeless.

Beatrice and I stood open-mouthed.

"Never seen Tunguska war dragons before, then?" said Shadwell. "You've got a treat in store! Now, if these children move, Noah, I command you to shoot — just try not to kill them."

Then, to my horror, Shadwell grabbed Torcher, who had gone limp in my arms at the sound of the whistle, and proceeded to bind his feet and tie his jaws shut with a length of thick rope. Soon our beloved chick was a bundle of ropes, and all he could do was growl and whip his tail back and forth when he finally came to again.

"Please!" begged Beatrice. "Don't tie him so tightly!"

"Why not?" said Shadwell. "He's just a dumb dragon. I'll tie him even more tightly if you don't shut up!"

Beatrice didn't say anything more. She bit her lip, and a tear ran down her cheek.

"Now, missy," said Shadwell, "you get up into that howdah with Noah — me and Flitz will take this other dragon with young Daniel."

When we didn't move, he casually pulled a pistol from his pocket.

"Come on, up you get, you brats," he said. "Don't you want to see your darling parents again?"

Beatrice and I looked at each other with wide eyes. So Alexandra *had* kidnapped our parents, and undoubtedly the other missing dragonologists as well.

Shadwell laughed at our shocked expressions, and Beatrice shot him a filthy look.

Unwillingly obeying Shadwell's orders, we climbed up into the howdahs on the backs of the war dragons, and Noah Hayes and Shadwell followed us.

There were seats inside the howdah, and Shadwell gestured to me to sit on one, throwing me a large white fur.

"And good riddance to that stinking desert!" shouted Shadwell.

At a signal from their mahouts, the Tunguska dragons took off, but not before I had a chance to glance down to where Prince Ranjit stood, helplessly stooped over the dying naga, a look of torment on his face.

Chapter XV
THE ICE PALACE

Some humans are greedy for power; others are greedy for treasure.

In dealing with them, know the difference.

— Liber Draconis, 'Humanology:

Notes on Our Unscaly Friends'

At first I couldn't imagine why we needed the furs. As we flew over the Thar Desert, it was blazingly hot. Moreover, the black Tunguska dragons travelled with such speed that Shadwell closed the shutters to stop the wind from howling around us, and it became sweltering inside the howdah. We struck north-east, crossing first over the wide desert, then a forest, which I could just see through a crack in the howdah. But as the day wore on, I stopped looking and fell into a fitful sleep. When I woke, day had turned into evening. I looked out to see that we were heading towards some enormously high, snowy mountains. I was thankful for the fur and pulled it around me.

Shadwell, who had pulled his own fur tightly round himself, had been splitting his time between dozing, drinking large glugs of liquor from a hip flask and counting out money, which he kept in a large wallet. He waved at me with his gun.

"Welcome to the Himalayas," he said. "The roof of the world."

I had thought that the Tunguska dragons would need to rest at night — even Uwassa couldn't fly on and on like this — but they flew without stopping into the cold and darkness. Despite the fur, my teeth chattered. By daybreak, my arms and legs felt stiff and sore.

"We'll have to toughen you up a bit, boy," laughed Shadwell. "Put you out with the driver. That'll get some frost in your bones."

The dragons were flying more slowly now that the sun had come up, and Shadwell threw open the shutters. A marvellous sight greeted my eyes. Few people other than dragonologists could ever have seen the wonders of the Himalayan Mountains from the air, and I gasped. We were flying down a long valley that had a glacier at the bottom of it.

"Let's see how smart you are, then," said Shadwell, "What do you think that is?" he asked, pointing to a

cone-shaped mountain higher than the rest. I shook my head dumbly. "That's Mount Everest, that is. The tallest mountain in the world."

"Is that where we're heading?" I asked.

"Not quite," said Shadwell. "We're going to that mountain on our left. In these parts it's known as Gyachung Kang. But I prefer to think of it as Mount Gorynytchka."

By now the dragons were wheeling downwards into a glacial valley that lay to one side of Gyachung Kang.

Below us, there seemed to be some sort of structure made of ice.

"This is the Ngozumpa Glacier. Beautiful, isn't it?" said Shadwell. "And it's deep in places, too. But that thing you're staring at wasn't made by nature, or man.

It was made by dragons, see. Carved out by dragon fire. And you haven't seen the half of it yet."

The war dragons swooped down and landed heavily on a large snowfield. The drivers, whose leather outfits were now covered in a layer of thick frost, walked nimbly up the dragons' spines and let down the rope ladders so we could disembark.

Still wearing our furs, Beatrice and I were ordered to walk along a path made of snow. Beatrice carried Torcher. I noticed that she was surreptitiously doing her best to loosen his tight bonds. My feet were freezing through the thin Indian slippers I was wearing, and I wondered how the drivers — or even the dragons — had managed to survive the journey. In front of us yawned a vast cave mouth cut into a wall of ice. Behind it, the cavern snaked down right into the heart of the glacier.

"Very grand, isn't it?" said Shadwell. "It took five dragons about two months, if I remember rightly. Now, get moving!"

Together we walked into the cave in front of Shadwell and Hayes, who was carrying the haversack that contained the treasures.

Then we turned a corner and saw the door.

Two enormous frost dragons sat on either side of the

Two enormous frost dragons sat on either side of the entrance.

entrance. Just like the black war dragons, their eyes were blank and dull. They reminded me of how Idraigir had looked earlier in the year when he had been under the control of Ignatius Crook, before we managed to free him. Dragons should be proud and free, but these were dazed and listless and sat almost as still as statues. Around each of their necks was a heavy chain, and between them, a massive iron door was supported by two enormous pillars that had been driven deep into the ice.

Shadwell smiled. He clapped his hands three times, and the frost dragons obediently pulled on the chains, causing the heavy doors to swing slowly open so that we could go inside.

As soon as the doors closed behind us, we felt a sudden rush of warmth. We were in a large hall lit by a multitude of coloured lamps. The walls were lined with ice pillars on either side, which were carved with amazingly detailed figures of dragons of many different species. But around each of their necks was a collar, and some of them were depicted fighting humans. Between the pillars hung magnificent tapestries, and these too showed scenes of dragons — pulling chariots, breathing flame in furnaces or hauling massive stones. Along the floor was a wooden walkway. Various iron doors and icy corridors led off from the hall, and I wondered which of them might be hiding our parents. I steadied myself. *I must not cry*, I thought. Flitz flew on ahead. The wooden walkway went right to the end of the hall, where there was another smaller pair of doors. They were ajar.

"I dare say that Miss Gorynytchka will be expecting us," said Shadwell.

Alexandra Gorynytchka sat on a magnificent dragon throne, her long black hair tumbling around her beautiful face. Like the rest of her remarkable palace, her throne was carved out of solid ice and draped with thick furs in order to make it comfortable. As we approached, Alexandra looked up and smiled. Hers was not a pleasant smile. Beside her, a young frost dragon had laid its head in her lap, and she was stroking it absent-mindedly. But like all the dragons we had seen that were under her control, its eyes were blank and faraway. With her other hand, she was fingering something that hung around her neck. I realised it was Saint Gilbert's Horn — one of the stolen treasures of the S.A.S.D.

So that's how she controls dragons! I thought.

Shadwell placed the haversack of treasures at her feet.

"Well, children, how lovely to see you both," said Alexandra mockingly. "It seems no time at all since we last met, wouldn't you agree? You *were* lucky to escape then, weren't you? I really thought that you and that meddlesome doctor would be buried alongside the Guardian."

"What have you done with our parents?" shouted Beatrice.

"Be quiet, child," said Alexandra icily. "Or you may regret it."

"I will not be quiet," insisted Beatrice. "I demand to know what you've done to them. And what have you done to these dragons?"

Alexandra laughed.

"Can't you guess?" she said, holding up Saint Gilbert's Horn. "I use this, with the help of a little dragon dust. Except for with my loyal Tunguska dragons. With them there is no need, for I raise them from the egg according to the ancient traditions of my family. They think I am their mother."

"So you want to control *all* dragons?" I said with a gasp.

"That would give me power indeed, wouldn't it?" said Alexandra. "Then I would be a true dragon queen!

There are — let me see — only around five thousand or so of them left in the world, according to — well, according to Dr. Ernest Drake, I believe. But no, I do not mean to control them all. Only the intelligent ones." She gave another laugh.

"But why are you kidnapping dragonologists?" I asked. "Are you trying to control them too?"

"Good heavens, no," said Alexandra. "I have no time for their ridiculous notions. But, although it pains me a great deal to admit it, I need their help. You see, there is a small matter of a dragon plague that has been accidentally unleashed," she continued. "It would not suit my plans for all dragons to die. And so I am 'recruiting' dragonologists to help me find a cure."

"You must be foolish to believe that our parents would ever do anything to help you!" exclaimed Beatrice.

Alexandra's eyes flashed.

"You dare to call *me* foolish, child?" she said.

She made a gesture, and the young frost dragon stood up almost mechanically and stalked towards Beatrice, growling horribly. But as it bared its teeth and reached its head back to lunge, Torcher wriggled violently, shook himself free of the ropes that Beatrice had loosened and leaped from her arms to defend her.

"No, Torcher!" cried Beatrice. "Stop!"

But it was too late. The frost dragon knocked Torcher sideways with a casual flick of his tail, sending him skidding across the ice floor. Then, as Torcher was scrambling to his feet, the frost dragon caught him full-on with a terrible frosty blast. The dragon chick was frozen so stiff that he could only blink his eyes.

"Please don't kill him!" screamed Beatrice.

"I shan't kill him," snapped Alexandra, "yet." She turned to look angrily at Shadwell.

"I thought I'd given orders for all dragons not directly under my control to be tied up securely," she said. "Take this one away, tie it up *tightly* this time, and make sure that there is no repeat performance."

Mumbling a grovelling apology, Shadwell dragged Torcher from the room. Flitz fluttered after him.

"There," said Alexandra. "I hope you have learned a lesson about what happens when I am not obeyed. Now, where were we? Oh, yes, you were telling me that your parents would never agree to help me cure the dragon plague. But what about you? Surely you will help me won't you?"

"Absolutely not!" I cried, but Alexandra just laughed.

"Oh, but you already have, you see," she said, bending to open the haversack at her feet.

She took the treasures in her hands. As she did so, her smile broadened.

"A book and a chalice," she said. " Now, let me see. You haven't brought me *two* of the *precious treasures* of the Secret and Ancient Society, have you? *Liber Draconis* and Saint Petroc's Chalice! Now, what would two naughty children be doing with such pretty, precious things? Taking them to Dr. Drake? To help him find a cure for the dragon plague? Am I getting warmer?"

Alexandra opened the book. As she did so, the smile left her face.

"Why are the pages blank?" she demanded, but neither of us answered.

"You know the secret, don't you?" she said. "You will tell me."

"We won't tell you anything," said Beatrice.

"That's what they *all* say," said Alexandra. "But they tell me everything in the end. You will too. The mere fact that I am keeping your parents prisoner will see to that. But no matter, for I have another use for you both. Once I have the famous Dragon Master himself imprisoned here, the threat of your demise will be enough to force him to find a cure for the dragon plague."

"But why imprison everyone?" I said. "Once he has these treasures, Dr. Drake is sure to find a cure wherever he is, and when he finds one, he will not deny it to any dragon, including yours."

"Yes, but that is *exactly* my problem. Dr. Drake will give the cure to *any* dragon that needs it," said Alexandra. "While *I* will make receiving the cure conditional on personal obedience to *me*!"

Alexandra rose. With a click of her fingers, she dismissed the frost dragon, which assumed a statue-like pose beside her throne. Then, carrying *Liber Draconis* and the chalice, she ushered us out of the throne room and into the hall. Noah Hayes followed.

Alexandra led us along a long corridor and down a twisting set of stairs. When we reached a heavy iron door she called out, *"Unicornucopia!"* The door swung open, and we entered a large ice chamber that was filled with a huge treasure hoard. I noticed Splatterfax, the war amulet of the Viking Rus, and the Spear of Saint George displayed among the treasures, both of which Alexandra had stolen from the Guardian. There were also many other swords, spears, cups and amulets lying

in profusion on the floor, not to mention a pile of gold and silver coins and gems of every colour that reached at least six feet high. On the very top of this pile lay what looked like a small pink worm with stubby wings. It was fast asleep. Alexandra turned to us.

"Once I had taken Saint Gilbert's Horn from that fool Ignatius Crook, this dragon was my first *real* prize," she said, gesturing towards the worm. "It is a *genuine* basilisk, one of the deadliest creatures alive. As a shape-shifter, it can take on the form of anything I command. It can change size too, and its attacks are always *fatal*! Now this deadly monster is the guardian of my treasures. It is a thousand times more powerful than the weak white worm I skewered near Wantley."

With a harsh cackle, she placed *Liber Draconis* and the chalice among the other treasures and turned to Noah Hayes.

"Wait here until I send Shadwell to you. And keep your gun trained on them at all times," she said, nodding in our direction. "If they make the slightest move to escape, shoot them."

Chapter XVI
A HAPPY REUNION

While much of the world's flora and fauna has now been understood,
in humanology the way still lies open for exciting new discoveries!
— Liber Draconis, 'Humanology:
Notes on Our Unscaly Friends'

Shadwell led us away from Alexandra's treasure chamber along the icy corridors and down several more flights of stairs. Noah followed. Finally, we stopped before another heavy metal door, with a grille, set into the ice wall.

"Welcome to your new home," said Shadwell with a leer. "Happy reunion!"

He took out a set of keys, selected one and unlocked the door. It swung open.

I stepped inside and immediately had one of those experiences in which time seems to move extremely slowly. First I caught sight of my mother. Then I saw my father. Their appearances hadn't changed at all since

"…And look how you've grown!"

I'd last seen them, except that the skin on their faces was darker, tanned by four years under the hot Jaisalmer sun. My mother turned towards me. Our eyes made contact, and she recognised me.

"Daniel!" she screamed. "Beatrice!"

She threw herself in our direction and flung her arms around us. My father looked at my sister open-mouthed. Then he flung himself towards us as well.

Behind us, the door slammed shut as Shadwell and Noah left, but we hardly noticed.

"Oh, my goodness," cried my mother, hugging us tight. "What on earth are you two doing here? Are you all right? And look at how you've grown!"

"My dear children," said Father, "it is a delight to see you — even in these unfortunate circumstances. But I must ask you, where is Dr. Drake?"

So, bit by bit, and in between lots of hugs, Beatrice and I explained everything that had happened since the Maharawal's telegram had arrived at Castle Drake.

"So the dragons themselves told you where to find the treasures, did they?" asked Father.

"Well, sort of," I explained. "But we couldn't have done it without Torcher."

"And who's Torcher?"

"He's a dragon chick," said Beatrice. "We raised him from the egg, but now Miss Gorynytchka has got him."

"It's all quite remarkable," exclaimed my mother. "I don't think even Dr. Drake was aware that *Liber Draconis* and Saint Petroc's Chalice held the key to the cure. He has been Dragon Master for such a short time that the dragons have had little chance to pass on all the knowledge that should now rightfully be his. And given recent events, they must be so wary about which dragonologists can really be trusted."

"Yes," agreed my father. "It is a great honour that they came to you children for help. I am so proud of you! But tell us, why did you bring the chick all the way here?"

"Because he can help us read *Liber Draconis*," I started to explain, but just at that point, Beatrice burst into tears.

"Oh, Mummy, I'm so scared!" she cried. "What if Miss Gorynytchka finds out how to read the book? Then she will have even more power over the dragons. And what will she do with poor Torcher? Surely he'll die if he's kept frozen for too long."

"Now, now," said my mother, patting Beatrice's hand. "We'll think of something, won't we, John?"

"Of course!" said my father. "We must find a way to

steal both Torcher and the treasures back and take them to Dr. Drake!"

"And we've got to get Saint Gilbert's Horn back, too," I said. "That way, Alexandra won't be able to control dragons quite so easily."

But the big question was how we were going to do it, locked as we were in a prison below the ice palace, with not even so much as a toothpick to help us get out...

Some hours passed, and then we heard Shadwell's voice in the corridor.

We stopped talking. The door opened. To my amazement, in walked Nia, followed by Dominique and Bernard Gamay. Shadwell stood in the doorway, rubbing his hands.

"You're going to find it a bit crowded," he said. "But Miss Gorynytchka ordered some special quarters to be prepared for Dr. Drake, so we needed to free up some space. It's a shame I can't stay long. I love it when old friends meet under difficult circumstances. But I have an important job to do, tracking down a friend of yours. It's time Dr. Drake found out just who Alexandra has as her house guests, don't you think?" Shadwell leaned into the corridor. "Noah! In here," he shouted.

Noah Hayes stepped into the cell, carrying a gun as

usual. He strode to one side of the room and just stood there, arms crossed, his face blank of all expression, as before.

Nia's mouth hung open.

"Remember, Noah," said Shadwell, "you are their guard now. You *will* shoot them if they try to escape. That's a command."

Noah raised his gun and pointed it in our direction. Shadwell gave a laugh and was gone.

Nia ran over to her father and threw her arms around his neck. "Daddy!" she cried.

Noah frowned. "Go away," he said. He sounded like an automaton. He pushed her away when she tried to hug him.

Nia bit her lip. "Daddy!" she said. "What's gotten into you? It's me, Nia. Don't you recognise me?"

"Hush," said Noah. "Noah's busy."

"Alexandra has hypnotised him, Nia," said Beatrice gently.

"I can see that," said Nia, promptly bursting into tears.

"Don't worry," I said, leading her away to sit in another corner of the cell with Beatrice. "We'll think of something. He is quite all right otherwise."

Meanwhile, Mademoiselle Gamay was filling my

parents in on the events that had befallen her.

"*C'était affreux!*" she exclaimed. "We were kidnapped by Shadwell and his thugs! They dressed as policemen and took us by surprise. Beatrice and Daniel managed to escape with Torcher, and young Darcy too. He ran off into the forest, but Nia and I were not so fortunate. Shadwell drove us to a warehouse somewhere, where one of Alexandra Gorynytchka's war dragons came to fetch us. By that time, more of her thugs had captured my brother, Bernard, and the French Dragon Master in Paris. Panthéon managed to rescue the French Dragon Master but, in doing so, he got captured himself. I suppose they will have brought him here, too, if he was still alive. He was very badly wounded."

"Poor Panthéon!" exclaimed Beatrice. And she explained to Mademoiselle Gamay Panthéon's part in our own escape from Paris.

"Did you manage to find Dr. Drake?" she asked.

"No," I said. "We got as far as the Thar Desert, but then Shadwell captured us, too. We met the Maharawal's nephew, Prince Ranjit, who told us that Dr. Drake is at the Hong Wei Temple, trying to help the monks find a cure for the *lung*. But the moment he finds out where we are, he is bound to begin a rescue attempt."

"Non!" exclaimed Mademoiselle Gamay. "He mustn't! It would be a trap!"

"And that's why we *must* escape," I said.

"So what we need to decide," said Beatrice, looking pointedly at Noah Hayes, "is what we are going to do about Noah. We've got to do SUM-thing, haven't we?"

Suddenly I knew what she meant. For earlier in the year, I had myself been hypnotised, and Dr. Drake had cured me by making me do no end of complicated mathematical sums.

"Er, yes," I said. "Hey, Nia, didn't you say that you were hypnotised once like me?"

"Well, yes I was," said Nia. She was catching on to our plan, too.

"How did they cure you?"

"Well, Conchita — that's the Mexican lady who brought me up on our ranch — hummed an old Spanish dragon chant to me, while Daddy made me do a whole mess of math. Now I can do my times tables quicker than Wyatt Earp can draw on the Clantons."

"Can you remember the chant?"

"Well, it kind of went, *'Bantale, bantale, bantale, bantale, bantale,'* over and over again, softly. I'll give it a shot on my daddy and see if it helps cure him."

"Brilliant," said my father. "Meanwhile, Beatrice and Daniel can try some, er, maths."

So the three of us went over and sat down next to Noah.

"Mr. Hayes?" I said. "Nia here says that you are very good at maths. I want to explain something to my family, and I wondered if you could help me. If Jamal flew us from Paris to Clermont-Ferrand in seven hours and the distance was two hundred and fourteen miles, then I was wondering what speed Jamal would have managed to fly at?"

"Noah can tell us. Can't you, Noah?" said Beatrice.

Noah looked at us suspiciously, as though he was trying to work out whether it was all right to tell us or not. Then he said, "Thirty miles per hour."

"Thank you!" said Beatrice. "That's very kind. You know, one of Jamal's wings measured eight feet, so what would his wingspan have been?"

"Sixteen feet."

We all grew excited apart from Noah, who looked confused. But I knew that we had to work fast, both for our own sakes and for the sake of Dr. Ernest Drake.

Luckily, Noah continued to be our chief guard over the next few days, and we all took turns asking him increasingly difficult mathematical questions, while Nia stood next to him, whispering the words of the chant. By the third day, Bernard had spent most of the morning asking, "What's one hundred and thirteen point four multiplied by seven? One hundred divided by eight? Twenty-nine million, seven hundred and eleven thousand, one hundred and thirteen plus thirty-eight thousand, nine hundred and ninety-eight? The square root of sixty-four multiplied by the square of eight?"

To which Noah gave out the answers, "Seven hundred and ninety-three point eight. Twelve point five. Twenty-nine million, seven hundred and fifty thousand, one hundred and eleven. Five hundred and twelve."

At the beginning of the fourth day, Noah looked the same initially, but after about half an hour, he put down his gun, and looked up at us with a puzzled expression on his face.

"Nia, baby!" he whispered. "Is that you?"

"Daddy!" cried Nia. "Oh, Daddy, Daddy, Daddy!" And she put her arms around him and hugged him as though she'd never get the chance again.

My parents shook Noah's hand warmly. "Good to have you back with us, Mr. Hayes," said my father, and we all agreed.

"But what are we all doing here?" asked Noah. "You'll all have to fill me in. I'm afraid my memory is more than a little blank in places. I can remember going out to the Thar Desert on a camel, then you all asking me math questions, but nothing much in between."

We explained the situation to him.

"We have to get out of here, Noah," said my father. "You must pretend to be hypnotised for a little while longer. Can you do that? We need you to help us plan our escape."

Noah nodded. "You've got it!" he said. "I'm on the case."

"You don't know if they've already discovered that Dr. Drake is at Hong Wei Temple, do you?" I said.

"No, I don't," he said. "Let me see what I can find out."

For the next few days, Noah pretended to guard us. The rest of the time, he did what he could to find out about the layout of Alexandra's Ice Palace without raising any suspicion.

The news wasn't good.

"Is there a way out of here?" asked Beatrice.

Noah thought. "On foot? No way!" he said. "There are glaciers and mountains for maybe hundreds of miles. You wouldn't survive five minutes in those conditions."

"So how do people get in and out?"

"On dragons," said Noah. "The big black Tunguska variety, mostly. The ones you all came in on yourselves. But Alexandra has a lot of other dragons under her control now. And there are more flying in every day."

"Alexandra must need a lot of dragon dust if she's taming so many dragons," said Bernard Gamay. "And the effects of Saint Gilbert's Horn aren't permanent. Where does she get it from, I wonder? And where does she keep it? If we can interfere with her supply, then we'll stand a much better chance of getting out of here."

"I don't know where she keeps it," said Noah. "I've only seen the main part of the palace, the dragon pens and the prison area, which is around here. But I have found out some more about the plague itself, and it seems that it was Alexandra herself who caused it. Somehow she managed to get her hands on an ancient vial that contained a powder that is deadly to dragons. She decided to experiment with it and, at first, because it produced only a mild sickness, she thought it had lost its potency. But now it has developed into something that threatens the existence of dragons everywhere."

"That woman is evil personified!" said my mother angrily, and we all agreed. "We must do something to stop her."

That night when he returned, Noah gave us a wink as he opened the door. "I have a surprise for you," he said, and with that, Torcher came scampering in.

"Oh, my, oh, my!" exclaimed Nia.

"Torcher!" Beatrice and I cried in unison.

Beatrice, Nia and I all threw ourselves at Torcher, hugging him and patting him. He jumped up at us and waggled his tail from side to side, looking none the worse for having been frozen.

"Good old Torcher!" I said. "But how on earth did you rescue him?"

"I found him in a corner of one of the dragon pens," said Noah. "But I had a helping hand when it came to rescuing him — from your French dragon friend Panthéon."

"Panthéon!" exclaimed Mademoiselle Gamay. "Is he all right?"

"Just about," said Noah. "The Tunguska dragon dust Alexandra is using to tame the other dragons has no effect on gargouilles, but he has been pretending to be hypnotised just like me. He believes a group of his loyal gargouilles may have followed him here and may be waiting outside the palace to help him escape whenever there is an opportunity. Panthéon is adamant that we must not leave here without the treasures. He told me that the Society of Dragons is relying on us. We must not let such powerful objects remain in the hands of someone who is an enemy of dragons everywhere."

"We'll do our best," said Beatrice.

"We'll have to," said Noah. "And fast, because I'm afraid that, whether we know the full layout of this place or not, we're going to have to make our escape attempt as soon as possible."

"Why's that?" asked Mademoiselle Gamay.

"I overheard some of the dragon mahouts. The war party is setting off for an attack tomorrow night. They must have found out the whereabouts of Dr. Drake and the location of Hong Wei. They were discussing Shadwell's instructions."

"What instructions?" I asked.

"Very simple ones," he said. "'Capture Drake. Leave no others alive'. Once she has the doctor in her clutches, she will force him to help her by holding you hostage and threatening to kill you unless he cooperates." We all looked suitably worried. "Cheer up," continued Noah. "There is one other thing I have discovered that might help us. Something remarkable."

"What's that?" my father asked.

"You know that Alexandra's own Tunguska dragons are not under the influence of dragon dust, don't you?" said Noah.

"Yes," said my father. "They obey her because she raised them and trained them herself."

"Yes, but that's just it. She did not personally train them all," said Noah. "There are too many Tunguska dragons for that. Nearly all the ones here are under the control of their own dragon mahout."

"The drivers!" I exclaimed.

"Yes," said Noah. "Now, most species of dragon — wyverns, *lung*, Europeans and so on — get much more intelligent as they get older. But because the Tunguska dragons have always been kept in captivity, their intelligence has been stunted. They can barely speak at all, and so each dragon mahout communicates with his dragon using a simple series of gestures. A prod behind the ear means up; a tap on the head means down. A jab in the back of the neck means 'Attack!' The rest is done with the reins."

"So anyone could control them," said my father. "Or at least anyone who knows the commands."

"Not quite," said Noah. "They only obey the mahouts, but the thing is, they recognise them not so much by their appearance as by their smell. All the mahouts' uniforms are washed in a special mixture of perfumes and herbs, which the dragons associate with them."

"So that's why the dragon mahout who brought me here smelled of spearmint!" I said.

"And mine too," said Beatrice. "I thought it was to cover up bad body odour!"

"Well," said Noah, "by my reckoning, if we steal the mahouts' uniforms, we might, just might, be able to fool the dragons into obeying us."

"It's risky," said my father.

"Very risky," said Noah. "But the most risky part of all is that the mahouts are quite small. Which means that the only ones who could easily pass for them would be—"

"The children," said my mother, looking shocked.

"Don't worry," I said. "We've ridden dragons before, haven't we, Bea?"

Beatrice nodded and gave me a thumbs-up.

It was time to perfect our escape plan.

Chapter XVII
ESCAPE

Do your best to conserve and protect any young humans in your care,
but do not worry about them unduly; they are neither rare nor unusual,
and there is no chance of them becoming extinct.
— Liber Draconis, 'The Humanology Handbook'

Our escape plan required that we split into three groups. First, Nia and Mademoiselle Gamay were going to accompany Noah to the mahouts' living quarters to steal three fur-lined uniforms, caps and pairs of goggles.

"It shouldn't be too difficult," said Noah. "The mahouts work in shifts, so it should be several hours before they notice the uniforms have gone."

My father and I had the more dangerous task of stealing back *Liber Draconis* and Saint Petroc's Chalice from the Treasure Room. First, my father asked Noah to help us prise a large mirror off the wall of the bathroom next to our cell.

"Why do we need this?" I asked him.

"According to Dr. Drake, it's the only *genuinely* reliable technique for dealing with basilisks," said my father. "Luckily, it seems that Alexandra hasn't heard of it. As I'm sure you know, basilisks have a fatally venomous bite. The trick to remember is that they always attack the one thing they regard as the most dangerous, so if you hold a mirror up to them, they will judge their own reflection the most dangerous and attack that. Let's hope that will keep the creature occupied for long enough to let us retrieve the treasure."

Meanwhile, Beatrice, my mother and Bernard had three tasks. Noah had discovered that the Ice Palace was heated by coal and that Alexandra had a whole year's supply stored in a series of bunkers beneath the palace. So first they were going to take Torcher and create a diversion by setting fire to the tapestries in the main hall. Then they were going down to set fire to the coal store, and finally they were going to find and free Panthéon. When all our tasks were done, we were going to make our way to the dragon pens, where Noah would hold off the guards using his gun while we donned the mahouts' uniforms and flew the dragons out, doing whatever damage we could on the way.

It seemed a very long shot, but it was the only one we had.

Noah looked out of the door and checked that there was no one in sight. Then he, Mademoiselle Gamay and Nia set off down the corridor.

Next, my mother, Beatrice and Bernard left with Torcher.

"Good luck!" I said, giving Beatrice and my mother a hug.

They smiled determinedly back at me.

Finally, my father and I stepped out into the corridor and headed for the Treasure Room. This part of the palace seemed as empty as it had when we had first arrived; there were no guards here.

"Perhaps Miss Gorynytchka is placing a little *too* much faith in her prize acquisition," said my father as we approached the door of the treasure room. "We shall see."

He held up the mirror in front of him, while I stood by the side of the door and cried, *"Unicornucopia!"* just as I had heard Alexandra do.

The door swung open. My father inched his way inside, using the mirror as a shield. I peered round the door. In front of the heap of treasure, I could see what appeared to be a baby yak. If it really was a yak, I thought, then it had most likely been placed there as food for the basilisk. If not, it might be the basilisk itself.

Suddenly, a golden statue of a snake coiled around a tree morphed itself into a cockatrice, and then into something that appeared to be a small but powerful wyvern. It was the basilisk, and it swivelled round to stare at the mirror.

"Quick! It's seen you!" I cried. With that, my father darted to one side, leaving the mirror propped against the ice wall. The wyvern looked towards Father for a second before turning back to gaze at its own reflection. Then it immediately morphed itself into a baby moth dragon and advanced towards the mirror, baring its fangs and hissing and spitting for all it was worth.

"Now, Daniel!" cried my father.

We dashed into the middle of the room and looked around hastily. I quickly spied Saint Petroc's Chalice and grabbed it, but I could not see *Liber Draconis* anywhere. I climbed frantically to the top of the huge pile of treasure.

"We must be quick!" cried my father. Behind him, I could see the basilisk was entirely focused on its own image in the mirror, as though it had decided to try and hypnotise itself. Meanwhile the poor, panicked yak had

The hydra struck the mirror a single blow...

begun to run round and round in circles. It was then that I saw *Liber Draconis*, near the bottom of the pile of treasure. The yak had been obscuring it as it cowered away from the basilisk, which was now readying itself for an attack on the mirror, changing form every few seconds — from cockatrice to wyvern, from wyvern to hydra, from hydra to marsupial to dragon shapes that I had never seen before.

"I've got it!" I cried, just as the dragon became a hydra again, all three heads hissing horribly as it propelled itself forwards towards the mirror. I grabbed *Liber Draconis*, and my father grabbed me. We both ran for the door.

The hydra struck the mirror a single blow with one of its heads, shattering it into thousands of pieces. As we slammed the door shut behind us, I was amazed to see the dragon almost blind in its fury, its heads twisting and turning crazily from one piece of mirror to another as if it could see a deadly enemy in each one. Then we headed as fast as we could towards the place where Noah had told us the dragon pens could be found. As we ran along the corridor, I noticed a trickle of water running along the floor. That meant that Beatrice, my mother and Bernard must have succeeded in setting fire not only to the tapestries in the main hall but also to the year's supply of coal in the bunkers beneath us. If that were the case, it was only a matter of time before large sections of the palace melted away entirely. I earnestly hoped they'd managed to find Panthéon.

Just at that moment, I heard a familiar gurgling, high-pitched roar coming from somewhere ahead of us. It *was* Panthéon, and he was summoning his loyal gargouilles down out of the mountains to fight! As if in answer, a much louder and deeper roar of anger echoed round the palace. I wondered if it was an alarm, for immediately a number of men came running down the corridor towards us. My father and I dodged down a side corridor and through a door, which we shut behind us, wedging the handle with a crate.

I turned and gasped.

We were in the corner of a vast ice cavern that contained some twenty black Tunguska war dragons, which stood in a menacing ring around a smaller group of three frost dragons. The frost dragons were looking back at them with bold defiance. Smoke rose to the roof and, in the centre of it all, on a tall plinth, stood Alexandra Gorynytchka, holding Saint Gilbert's Horn to her lips as though she were about to blow a note. By her side was Shadwell, next to a large stone storage jar that was shaped like a dragon's head. Alexandra spotted us and a look of fury passed across her face. She shouted an instruction to one of the Tunguska dragons, which instantly turned and spat out a jet of flame in our direction. We leaped aside and, using a row of crates for shelter, ran through another door, leaving the chamber just before a further jet of flame came spouting towards us. We fled along another corridor and finally reached the area where Noah had told us the dragon pens were located. By now, we were splashing as we ran, for there was perhaps half an inch of water on the floor.

The cave that held the dragon pens was circular and did not have a roof. High above, I could see the starry sky and the white tops of the Himalayan Mountains. Along the walls hung huge grilled iron gates set deep into the ice, and it was behind these that the black Tunguska dragons were stabled. One of the gates had been opened. Beside it, I could see Noah, Mademoiselle Gamay and Nia, while out of the gate came three war dragons, howdahs fixed onto their backs. Nia was already dressed in the uniform of a dragon mahout and had picked up a dragon ankus. Two other uniforms lay on the ground nearby. I began to believe for the first time that our plan was actually going to work.

As Noah covered some guards with his gun, Mademoiselle Gamay and Nia began climbing up the ladder into the howdah of the first war dragon.

"Take the middle dragon," Noah called to us. "Put your uniform on first." He indicated one of the sets of clothes on the floor. Hastily I pulled them on and picked up the dragon ankus that lay alongside them. My father took the treasures. Then we both rushed over to the second war dragon and began climbing up the ladder. The dragon turned its head towards us.

"Praisich boyar!" I said.

But the dragon did not reply. When I reached the howdah, I climbed round it, making my way along the dragon's spines to the saddle, and took the reins in my hands.

Just then my mother, Beatrice and Bernard Gamay burst into the cave. At first I couldn't see if Torcher was still with them. But as three men ran through the door behind them, it was soon clear that Torcher was very much present, as he leaped from Beatrice's arms and stood between her and the men. A jet of flame spurted out of Torcher's mouth, causing the men to jump back. Noah gestured to Beatrice to put on the third uniform, which she did as quickly as she could, while Torcher kept the men at bay. However, his fire did not last, and it was not long before they were advancing again.

The ladder of the third war dragon hadn't yet been lowered. I saw Beatrice pick up her dragon ankus and tap it on the floor in front of the dragon — just as Noah had instructed us — and the great beast lowered its head to the floor obediently. Nimble as a cat, Beatrice leaped onto the dragon's snout, stepped between its horns and ran down its neck to the howdah to lower the ladder.

Meanwhile, the three guards had managed to overcome Noah, and he was trying to fight them off. He knocked one of them over backwards but then fell over himself. He barely managed to roll clear as the ice wall next to him was suddenly blasted apart in a burst of flame. An enormous black dragon stepped through the gap and advanced towards Noah, letting out a deafening roar. My dragon was closest to it, so I pulled on my reins and lightly prodded my dragon in the back of the neck with the ankus. For a moment, nothing happened. Then my dragon let out a bellowing roar and turned towards the newcomer, ready to fight. I desperately hoped that my uniform had flameproof properties. Otherwise, even if we bested our combatant, I could still be fried to a crisp.

Meanwhile, my mother and Bernard had climbed up to the howdah of the third war dragon behind Beatrice.

"Get airborne!" I cried to the others. "Father and I will rescue Noah!"

"*Gerupthar!*" cried Beatrice, prodding her dragon behind its ears.

"*Algrai!*" cried Nia, doing the same. "Yee-haw! *Algraiiiii!*"

With two mighty leaps, Beatrice and Nia's dragons took off, beating their wings to gain height as they flew up into the cavern. Beatrice's dragon flew higher and was circling round and round the inside wall of the cave, while Nia's dragon was hovering almost motionless. In front of us, Noah and Torcher were trying to reach my father and me, but the angry dragon was in the way, roaring ferociously. And behind it, Alexandra and Shadwell appeared, followed by even more men and dragons.

"Kill him!" screamed Alexandra, pointing towards Noah, at which the huge Tunguska turned and lunged for him. Somehow Noah managed to grab the dragon's snout as it tried to bite him. He swung himself up onto its head, leaped along its neck and shoulders, then made a desperate jump to catch the trailing ladder of Nia's dragon as it hovered above him.

I leaned out over the edge of our howdah, searching for Torcher. Suddenly I saw him, trying to hold off three small dragons that were advancing on him with outstretched claws.

I couldn't see any way of reaching him, and my heart sank. At that exact moment, an excited yell sounded from high above us. It was Beatrice, and soon her voice was joined by others as a great cheer went up.

"*Panthéon! Vive Panthéon!*" cried Bernard Gamay. "*Et les gargouilles! Vive les gargouilles!*"

Panthéon had come to the rescue. Now he and his loyal gargouilles were diving down into the cavern. Flame and fighting dragons were everywhere. Shards of ice flew up around us as whole walls of the palace began to cave in, engulfing Alexandra and her black dragons in a huge torrent of ice, steam and black smoke. Flames poured from several holes in the ground beneath the cave. My dragon swung its head fiercely, butting the huge Tunguska's head out of the way. Then it stepped forward, beating its wings and circling upwards through the melee.

Soon we had crested the roof of the crumbling

cavern and were heading up into the night sky, past the other two dragons, who were waiting, perched precariously on the lip of the cave. Then Panthéon appeared, hovering at my side.

"Torcher!" I cried. "Torcher is still down there!"

Panthéon swooped back down, then reappeared just a few minutes later, with Torcher clutched in his claws. I could not believe it! He passed the little dragon to Mademoiselle Gamay and cried out, *"À l'est!"*

"East!" shouted Bernard. "We must fly east!"

I pulled on the reins to turn my dragon in the direction Panthéon had indicated. The others did likewise, and we flew as one away from Gyachung Kang, the shouts and roars gradually fading behind us. Soon we had passed the slopes of Mount Everest and were flying onwards in a huge V-formation, our three dragons following Panthéon, with the loyal gargouilles behind us. I guessed where we were heading.

"How long will it take us to reach Hong Wei?" I called back to my father, who was checking that the treasures remained undamaged.

"I'm not sure," he replied. "Let's just hope it's soon enough to save the *lung*."

Chapter XVIII
HONG WEI TEMPLE

Asian lung *are very wise, as they are fond of reminding*
all who have dealings with them.

— Liber Draconis, 'Key Features of Different Dragons'

I t took us three days of flying at top speed to reach
Hong Wei. We had taken two short rest breaks in
small valleys and, on the third day, found ourselves
soaring over a mountainous part of southern China.
During the journey I had not seen any dragons behind
us, but now I had a distinct sense that we were being
followed. As I looked back, Nia's dragon swooped in
nearer to mine.

"There are dragons on our tail," she said, pointing
towards some dark shapes in the distance. "From this
far off, I can't tell what species they are, but if they are
Alexandra's war dragons, I wonder why they haven't
attacked us yet."

"Perhaps they are waiting for reinforcements!" I

shouted back. We had no time to continue our conversation, for Panthéon, who was flying some distance in front, began to fly downwards towards a range of tall, conical hills. Our dragons followed in a steep dive and, as they did so, the dragons behind us put on a burst of speed to catch up. Close up, it became clear that they were undoubtedly Tunguska war dragons, although they were smaller than ours and weren't carrying howdahs. I could just make out a rider sitting on a saddle between the shoulders of the front dragon. It did not seem to be Alexandra although, at that range, it was difficult to tell.

I looked down. Below us, a mountain valley came into view, with a large temple at one end and, in front it, a

lake dotted with pagodas and ornate bridges.

Water poured from the lake over the edge of a cliff in a shimmering cascade. As we approached, I could just make out a set of steps that led up the cliff, behind the cascade, and emerged near the lakeside. And climbing — almost leaping — rapidly up the steps was a sprightly old gentleman who could only have been dear old Dr. Drake himself.

I felt like calling out, but I knew he would not hear me. I could see Beatrice looking down from her dragon, waving frantically.

A horn blew then — a long, loud note — and a lot of people, many of them dressed in orange robes, began to scamper around the temple complex. A young Chinese woman and an old man with white hair came out of the temple and went down to the lake to greet Panthéon, who had already landed, while others ran back to the main temple building.

Behind me, the black dragons were drawing ever closer, and now I could clearly see Shadwell in the saddle of the first dragon. He flew nearer until he was just out of flame range.

"Hey, Daniel!" he called. "That isn't you in that mahout outfit, is it?"

I did not reply.

"I just wanted to say thanks for showing us the way to Hong Wei!" Shadwell continued.

"I thought you already knew the way," I cried. "You said you were planning to attack."

"Oh, but we are," he replied sarcastically. "We knew *roughly* where it was. Now we know *exactly*. So don't worry. The attack will still take place. As you can imagine, Miss Gorynytchka is breathing fire herself over how you've damaged her home. So she's really looking forward to it."

By now the lake was directly beneath us. Shadwell opened his mouth to speak again, but before he could say anything more, four deep-blue shapes burst from its surface and four magnificent Chinese *lung* leaped about seventy feet into the air to confront the war dragons. Shadwell immediately steered his dragon back over the cliff and the others followed. He turned round, gave a short, cruel laugh and then disappeared back in the direction from which he'd come.

I tapped my dragon gently on the head, and it swooped low to land in the area between the lake and the main temple buildings. I climbed down as quickly as I could and looked round to see Beatrice, already on the ground, cradling something in her arms.

"What's the matter?" I cried, rushing over to her.

"It's Torcher," Beatrice answered. "He's suddenly started coughing, and there's some yucky phlegm coming out of his mouth."

She held the dragon chick out to me. He looked very ill indeed and was having difficulty breathing.

"Do you think it's the sickness?" I said. I was horrified.

"He must have caught it in the Thar Desert," said Beatrice.

Just then, Dr. Drake came hurrying up, accompanied by the young woman. Behind them, the old man followed with Panthéon.

"Daniel! Daniel!" cried the doctor. "I thought my eyes were deceiving me, but it seems not. And are those your parents I see, and the Gamays, and Nia and her father too?"

"I'm afraid Alexandra Gorynytchka is not far behind us," I said. "She has been keeping us all captive in her ice palace in the Himalayas, but we managed to escape."

"Goodness me, what a tale you must all have to tell, but for now it must wait while we attend to Torcher. Another case of the sickness, I fear. Miss Ta, a bottle of my linctus, please." And with that, the dark-haired girl handed Dr. Drake a small bottle filled with a viscous green liquid, which he administered immediately by manfully pouring it down the dragon chick's throat. Almost at once, Torcher began to breathe more easily and had soon fallen into a peaceful sleep in Beatrice's arms.

"Unfortunately," Dr. Drake said, "my linctus is not able to cure this new form of dragon plague, but it can slow down the development of the symptoms. It is imperative that we devise a cure, but so far, nothing we have tried seems to work."

By now we had been joined by the rest of our group, and once the adults had finished shaking hands, I took *Liber Draconis* and Saint Petroc's Chalice from my father and handed them to Dr. Drake.

"Perhaps these might help, sir," I suggested.

"But where on earth did you find them?" he asked. "And how in the name of all the blue dragons did you get them here?"

So we explained as quickly as possible all that had happened since Dr. Drake had left on the Dragon Express, with everyone chipping in to tell their part of the extraordinary story.

"This is quite amazing," said Dr. Drake when he had heard everything we had to say. "I can't believe that the treasures were actually at the S.A.S.D. headquarters all along. I wonder what other secrets the Society of Dragons still has to share with me. But you must forgive me. In listening to your story, I have forgotten my manners. I would like to introduce the Master of Hong Wei Temple and my dear dragonological friend Miss Ta. They have been helping me care for the Chinese *lung* that are now falling sick with this plague."

At this, the old man, who was dressed in long white robes, bowed, and the young woman, who was dressed all in blue, gave a nod and a smile.

"The ways of heaven are hard for mortals to understand," said the Master of Hong Wei, "for while it is useful to have dragons to fight battles, it is better to have dear friends bring the weapons needed to win the war. I am happy to meet you."

"Indeed," exclaimed Dr. Drake. "Now let us make haste — work with *Liber Draconis* and Saint Petroc's Chalice must begin at once!"

"But what about Alexandra Gorynytchka?" said my father. "Now that she knows we are all here, she is even more likely to mount an attack."

"I'm sure she will," said Dr. Drake. "And soon. So it is imperative that some of us prepare to defend Hong Wei while others concentrate on finding the cure."

"Beatrice and I have already discovered the secret of how *Liber Draconis* works," I said. "Torcher helped us."

"You must tell me more," said Dr. Drake. "But first let me discuss the matter of temple defences with the others. We have much to do and little time. And Beatrice, I think Miss Ta should take Torcher to the infirmary. He will be more comfortable there."

Once the adults had received their instructions, Dr. Drake returned to where Beatrice, Nia and I were waiting.

"Tell me what you have discovered," said Dr. Drake.

"Well, the pages of *Liber Draconis* appear blank until they are exposed to dragon fire," said Beatrice, and she explained what Torcher and Uwassa had helped to reveal. "To read the whole thing, you need to find the right species of dragon."

"And even then, the words are like some sort of riddle," I continued.

"Typical of a dragon," said Dr. Drake, shaking his head. "But then, of course, the two of you are experts at solving riddles," he continued, beaming at Beatrice and me. "Let us go to the temple library, where we can consider what you have learned so far. Follow me."

It was true that we had worked out more than one such puzzle during our last adventure with the doctor, but my heart was heavy with responsibility as we trudged up the temple steps and into a circular room with a breathtaking view of the valley.

"As we said, we've only found two dragon species that reveal the book's writing so far," I began, handing both the book and the chalice to Dr. Drake. "They each revealed a part of what might be the recipe we need, as well as two terms: *Tears of Isis* and *brimstone*. The problem is that those terms don't match up with the words engraved around the rim of the chalice."

"Although we can guess what *sulphur* and *aqua* are," said Beatrice.

"Aha," said Dr. Drake, holding up the chalice and turning it in his hand. "The words around the rim are easy enough if you have studied the language of ancient Rome. They are in Latin, and they read: *sulphur*, which is the same in English; *antimonium*, or antimony; *aqua*, or water; and *verbena*, or vervain. Now, *Tears of Isis* is another name for the herb vervain, while *brimstone* is an old English name for sulphur."

"That's dandy!" exclaimed Nia. "We're halfway to finding the cure already!"

"Now, there are two more blank pages, so we need to find out which other dragon species can light them up,"

said Beatrice. "We know that it's not a hydra — Faki-Kifa-Kafi proved that.
But could a *lung* be one of the others?"

"That will be easy enough to find out," I said. "But there must be a fourth one."

"Perhaps the last dragon is a gargouille," said Panthéon, appearing in the doorway of the library. "Place the book on the ground, and we shall see."

We obeyed at once, and Panthéon blew a short burst of flame over it. To our relief, the words *Liber Draconis* sprang to life in orange letters on the cover.

"*Voilà!*" he said. "Now you only need one more dragon."

And with that, he gave a low, gargling roar, which was answered immediately by a loud splashing noise from the lake. As we turned to look, I saw one of the four magnificent blue *lung*, which we had seen earlier, emerge from the waters and step out onto the shore, its feathered tail curled behind it. It made its way sedately up the steps towards us until it was looking in through one of the arches in the library with eyes full of ancient wisdom.

Just then, the Master of Hong Wei joined us. "I see you have made the acquaintance of my old friend," he said. "Allow me to introduce Lung Hong, Dragon King of the Eastern Sea!"

"Allow me to introduce Lung Hong, Dragon King of the Eastern Sea!"

Beatrice and I bowed low before this majestic dragon.

"I am pleased to meet you," said Lung Hong. "As fresh rain from heaven is welcome to parched crops, so are new friends ever welcome to Lung Hong."

And with that, he blew a light breath of flame over the book, and a hint of green was added to the title on the cover.

Everyone watched, including the two dragons, as I bent down and opened the dragon diary to the pages that showed the chalices. Although the European and wyvern parts were missing, we could now read *Kohl* — in orange — and *Aqua* — in green — on two new images of the chalice.

"*Kohl* is another word for antimony," observed the Master of Hong Wei.

"And *aqua* is water, of course," said Nia.

Beneath each picture were the missing lines from the riddle, together with some instructions. At long last, we had the words of the cure before us. Put together with the lines that we had already read, they said:

> My first is in veins but not in blood,
> My second is in squawk but not in hoot.
> My third is in wise but not in fool,
> My fourth is in apple but not in fruit.

My fifth is a secret of mixing them well,
My sixth heats them up till they bubble and swell.
My seventh's a name that names me so well —
Recite it ten times for the bubbling to tell.
My eighth cools all in a babbling brook.
My ninth's where they hear, and then where they look.

In a chalice that is composed of 10 parts gold, 1 part
silver, and 1/16 part mercury, mix equal parts pure
water, vervain, sulphur and antimony according to the
above charm. This recipe shall be known as Aladdin's
Dragon Cure.

"Now I must leave you," said Dr. Drake. "The
Master and I need to go and help the others. Alexandra
Gorynytchka might attack at any moment, and we must
resist her at all costs. I will come back as soon as I can
to see how you are getting on. Until then, it is up to
you to do your best to work out what the riddle means."

"You can rely on us, sir," I said. "We will do our best."

"May heaven bring forth a beneficial result to your
efforts," said the Master of Hong Wei. And with that,
they left us alone.

We read the riddle again.

"Do you think we have to repeat this riddle over and over as a charm while mixing up the ingredients?" suggested Nia.

"I doubt it," said Beatrice. "There is almost always some scientific method to these old charms."

"I'd say the first four lines look just like a regular riddle," said Nia. "You have to spot letters in the first words that aren't in the second words, and put them together so they mean something."

"Yes," I said. "But it doesn't make sense after that."

"I know," said Nia. "But why don't we start with the first bit and see if we get anywhere?"

We all agreed, so we tried to work out which letters appeared only in the first word, but not in the second, and which words they might make in combination. After about half an hour, we had found a few words, like *snip* and *idea*, but they didn't seem to mean anything.

Then suddenly I saw the answer.

"I've got it!" I said. "It's just the first letter of the word that is important. *V. S. W. A. Veins, squawk, wise, apple.* Vervain, sulphur, water, antimony. That must be the order in which the materials should be mixed!"

"What about the next part?" asked Beatrice excitedly.

"Well, the fifth and sixth parts are simply saying that

all the ingredients must be mixed well and heated up until they bubble and swell," I said.

"And the seventh part has to do with how long you heat them for!" said Nia. "'For the bubbling to tell.'"

"Yes, but how long is that?" asked Beatrice.

"There's a name that must be recited ten times," I said.

"I knew it!" said Nia. "There *is* a magic word, after all." She thought for a moment. "No, that's not it," she said. "It's the *length* of the word that is important. Reciting it ten times isn't magic — it gives you the length of time you've got to let the mixture bubble for."

"And after that you simply cool the mixture in a bubbling brook, and then apply it," said Beatrice. "And of course! It must *not* be drunk. Listen: 'My ninth's where they hear, and then where they look.' You have to put it in the dragons' ears and eyes, a bit like eyedrops. Perhaps it would be destroyed if they simply ate it."

"You are both geniuses," I said, giving them each a hug. "But what on earth is the 'name that names me so well'?"

Which name could it possibly be? Whose name?

It came to me in a flash.

"I know!" I cried. "It's the name of the spell itself! Aladdin! The name is Aladdin!"

✳

We set off at once to tell Dr. Drake about our discovery and found him deep in conversation with three of the monks. He looked worried and kept glancing up towards the skies, where Panthéon was circling as a lookout.

"Well done!" shouted Dr. Drake once he had heard. "You must find Miss Ta and get her to take you straight to the monks' laboratory. They will have all the ingredients you need to mix up a batch of the recipe and see if it works."

We found Miss Ta down at the lake, teaching our parents and the Gamays how to ride *lung* dragons in preparation for the battle.

They were all delighted to hear the news of our breakthrough, and Miss Ta led us quickly past the temple buildings to one that sat on its own at the end of the lake. Inside, it was set up much as Dr. Drake's laboratory at the S.A.S.D., with lots of scientific equipment and a great many jars, bottles and dishes, not to mention countless pieces of jade and all sorts of precious stones.

Hardly hesitating, Miss Ta selected various jars and placed them before us.

"Here," she said. "Vervain. Sulphur. Antimony. And

something to mix them in. Don't touch the last two with bare hands. Water you can fetch from the lake."

And with that, she left us.

Beatrice had brought the chalice with us and placed it on the counter. Together, we started to measure out the ingredients while Nia went to fill up a pitcher at the waterfall. Then, holding our breath, we mixed them according to the recipe in *Liber Draconis*. What resulted was a bright red liquid, thick and sweet-smelling, which we carried reverentially over to the dragon infirmary. The moment of truth had arrived.

Torcher lay in a basket, still sleeping soundly. We took advantage of his inanimate state by pouring a small amount of the medicine into each of his ears. He woke up at once and began wriggling around with all his might and shaking his head. He made it extremely difficult to get any into his eyes by snapping at my hands, but eventually I managed to get a drop in each one, and he fell asleep again almost at once.

We relaxed. It had been easier than we had thought.

"Is he going to be all right now, do you think?" said Beatrice.

"*All* the dragons are going to be all right," I said determinedly.

"Just so long as Dr. Drake and the Master can fight off Miss Gorynytchka," said Nia.

She was right.

For even though it appeared that we had found a cure for the dragon plague, Alexandra Gorynytchka had so many Tunguska war dragons under her command that I really didn't see how we were going to survive her onslaught at all.

CHAPTER IX
THE BATTLE OF HONG WEI

Above all, be brave.
— Liber Draconis, 'Endnote'

Over the next few hours, Nia, Beatrice and I took turns mixing and administering the dragon cure to as many sick dragons as we could manage. Most of the sick *lung* patiently accepted the medicine, although some of them were a little squeamish about having the mixture poured into their eyes, and often with the larger creatures I had to stand on a chair to pour the drops in. However, none of them wriggled about as much as Torcher had.

During all of this time, Dr. Drake, the Master of Hong Wei and the others, with help from Panthéon and the Dragon Kings, were doing their best to prepare the temple against attack. Their task was not easy. The temple had been built perhaps a thousand years earlier and had never been conceived of as a defensive structure.

Although it was almost completely impregnable from attack from the valley below, because of the narrowness and steepness of the stairway that led up to it, it was extremely vulnerable to any kind of airborne attack. Additionally, there was the problem of finding enough healthy dragons to defend it. Of course, it went without saying that Panthéon and his valiant gargouilles would fight, as would the Tunguska dragons that we had freed from the Ice Palace. At first, Nia, Beatrice and I had naturally assumed that we would have to ride them into battle, too, but — to my great relief — my father explained that this would not be necessary.

"You children can take no part in the battle," he had said. "Things were different in the Ice Palace. We needed to escape, and there was no other way. Here, there is another way. Look!"

He gestured towards the three young monks I had seen Dr. Drake talking to earlier, who had now put on our scented uniforms and had already begun to work with the black dragons.

All the fit *lung* — including the four Dragon Kings, who normally lived in different parts of China but had come to Hong Wei Temple because of the emergency — were determined to fight, even though they were essentially peaceful creatures and, unlike the Tunguska war dragons, unable to fly. Lung Wei — the Dragon King of the Western Mountains — rose majestically out of the water and spoke for all of his kind when he declared, "Surely it is the will of heaven that all *lung* should join you to fight this human who has unleashed such a terrible scourge upon our kind. Our reasoning is plain: heaven smiles on those who work according to nature. Freedom is our nature. We will never give up our freedom, and so, for a time, we must give up our customary peacefulness and fight."

Dr. Drake and the Master bowed low to the Dragon King after he made his speech, and they thanked him, but even with the help of the Dragon Kings, I could not see how Dr. Drake's relatively small army could possibly be a match for Alexandra's force of powerful Tunguska war dragons.

✳

The rest of the day passed relatively uneventfully. Dr. Drake came to visit us in the infirmary, and we were pleased to report that even after just a few hours, many of the dragons were showing signs of recovery.

That night, despite my exhaustion, I slept only fitfully. I repeatedly dreamed of Alexandra riding a giant basilisk, brandishing *Liber Draconis* and cackling triumphantly.

At first light, just as we were preparing to mix up yet another batch of cure, I caught sight of two gargouilles returning to the temple. A few moments later, the warning horn began to blow. It could mean only one thing: Alexandra Gorynytchka's army of war dragons had been sighted. The attack on Hong Wei Temple was about to begin.

Beatrice, Nia and I were ordered to go into the main temple building — which was built mostly of stone. We found a window that looked down on the valley and, from this vantage point, we watched as most of the adults, dressed in a variety of flame-resistant armour, rushed out to mount the *lung*. The *lung* were going to fight from the lake, where they could use their water leap to greatest advantage. The gargouilles were already on the wing, circling above us, while the three war dragons and their monk mahouts were stationed on the edge of the cliffs above the cascade.

"Where's Panthéon? " I asked. "I can't see him among the other gargouilles."

"Me neither," said Beatrice.

Around the temple buildings, many of the other

dragon monks stood by, armed with wooden buckets filled with water, ready to put out fires, and with long staves in order to fend off the war dragons when they attacked. They didn't look as though they stood a chance. I squeezed Beatrice's hand. I wished that I had said something to our parents when I had still had time.

At first, everything was quiet after the horn blast. Then a tiny blue speck came fluttering over the lip of the cascade and flew towards us over the lake. It was Flitz! As he came nearer, it was clear that he too had fallen victim to the plague, for there was a distinct sound of coughing and his flight looked laboured and uneven. He flew once round the temple buildings before disappearing back in the direction from which he'd come.

Seconds later, we became aware of a distant hum that grew louder and louder until it turned into a roar. Then I saw them. At first they were like a distant black cloud, but as they came nearer, I counted at least thirty or forty war dragons with armoured drivers racing through the sky towards us.

"Now I know how Davy Crockett must have felt at the Alamo," declared Nia.

I laughed despite myself. "Let's just hope it doesn't

end the same way," I said.

Sitting astride the Dragon King of the Western Mountains, the Master of Hong Wei turned to Dr. Drake. "Surely even with heaven on our side, we cannot hope to defend ourselves against so many," he said.

"But they are Tunguskas," said Dr. Drake. "And therein lies their weakness!" He raised his voice: "Hear me, defenders of Hong Wei, dragons and humans alike! We stand here today at a crossroads in the history of dragonology. If Alexandra Gorynytchka triumphs on this day, her power will be dreadful. Under the threat of her dragon armies, both humans and dragons will cease to have the freedom we cherish as a right of all creatures. For that reason, this cannot be a battle that we lose. This must be a war that we win! Although it may seem as if we are fighting against insurmountable odds, Alexandra's war dragons have a vital weakness. Their sense and intelligence is so dulled by years of captivity that they respond only to the commands of their mahout. So when they attack, concentrate your efforts on unseating their riders. Do not hurt the dragons themselves, for, without its mahout, each dragon will have no reason to attack." He paused. "And now," he cried, "let them come! We are ready!"

A great cheer rang out among the defenders. "To the defence of Hong Wei!" they called.

I looked into the skies. By now, I could make out individual dragon mahouts. Alexandra Gorynytchka rode at the front of the attack, wearing a silver breastplate and carrying the Spear of Saint George high in her hands. Next to her came Shadwell.

"If Dr. Drake is right about aiming for the drivers, why the blazes don't we just use guns to defend ourselves?" said Nia.

"Because the monks don't have any guns," I said.

"Then I reckon we're done for," said Nia. "Know any good prayers?"

But then, to our great surprise, Panthéon flew up from behind the temple. With him were Idraigir and Uwassa, along with Faki-Kifa-Kafi, two other wyverns and five other European dragons.

Beatrice, Nia and I all cheered, while Idraigir waited as Dr. Drake climbed up on his back.

"Still say we're done for?" I said to Nia.

By now Alexandra and her war dragons were nearly upon us.

"Yeeeeeeeee-haaaaaaaaahhh!" screeched Alexandra as her dragon came swooping down and a great blast of flame belched out of its mouth.

"Now!" cried Dr. Drake, he and Idraigir rose into the air to confront her.

At once, Uwassa, Faki-Kifa-Kafi and the other flying dragons took to the wing, while the *lung* and their riders leaped high into the air, each doing its best to use jaw, claw or tail to topple the drivers of the Tunguskas, which now seemed to be everywhere. Panthéon led the gargouilles in a nimble diving attack to harry Alexandra's war dragons from above. Flames were erupting from every direction, making the airborne conflict difficult to see, but I did spot a leaping *lung* unseating one of Alexandra's mahouts, who tumbled down into the lake and was at once fished out and made prisoner by the angry monks. As the *lung* fell back towards the lake, I saw that my mother was riding it.

"Mother has got one!" I shouted. "Go on, Mother!"

Then I looked back towards the now riderless dragon to see whether Dr. Drake had been right. And indeed, without the mahout to command it, the Tunguska dragon continued to fly alongside its companions but showed no further inclination to breathe flame or attack.

No sooner had I witnessed that first brief victory than things took a turn for the worse. While Uwassa and

"Yeeeeeeeee–haaaaaaaaahhh!" screeched Alexandra…

Faki-Kifa-Kafi were making short work of protecting our left and right flanks. Idraigir had flown in to try to dislodge Alexandra from her war dragon. But she had managed to dodge him and had swung round so that the blast of flame that poured from her dragon's mouth seared through the sky in a huge arc, burning the arm of one of the monks. His *lung* instinctively turned in order to protect him, exposing its side in the process.

"Die, beast!" screamed Alexandra, plunging the Spear of Saint George deep into its exposed underbelly. Beside me, Beatrice let out a horrified cry as she watched the stricken *lung* plummet to earth, bucking its rider, who fell wide of the lake with a horrible thud and then lay still.

The rest of the *lung* retreated to the lake, and the black dragons reached the temple buildings, shooting out flames that set light to everything they touched. Immediately the monks rushed to put out the blazes, while Nia, Beatrice and I ducked back into the safety of our stone room. But it was not buildings that Alexandra wanted to destroy. The war dragons soon spun round and flew in a wide arc, running a gauntlet of diving gargouilles as they prepared for another attack.

As the war dragons closed in for a second time, Dr. Drake and the rest of the adults continued to resist them: Panthéon unseated one of the Tunguska mahouts on the second charge, as did Uwassa and Faki-Kifa-Kafi, who nearly managed to topple Shadwell into the bargain. Noah, who had a lasso that he kept whirling around his head, managed to catch a mahout and drag him off, so that he, too, fell into the water below. On the third charge, the Gamays got two more without taking any damage themselves. In fact, the battle was proving to be much more equal than I had expected. Only Alexandra seemed to have a deadly weapon, and she struck to the left and right with her spear, wounding and killing several *lung* and at least two gargouilles as she tried to find a way to get at Dr. Drake. Meanwhile, the Master of Hong Wei, who had performed *lung* leaps for far longer than anyone else, was showing his worth. He unseated two mahouts in one charge alone, and as each driver fell into the lake, we cheered.

But just after the fourth charge, I heard a clattering noise and felt a sudden, searing heat down the back of my neck. I spun round. It was Flitz! Somehow or other he had managed to fly in through one of the windows and had knocked over Saint Petroc's Chalice, spilling the precious cure across the floor.

Beatrice and Nia gasped, while I looked around for

something we could defend ourselves with. But Flitz, instead of attacking us, coughed loudly and began to flutter in the pool of dragon cure, like a robin taking a birdbath in a puddle. When his bath was done, he turned towards us, his eyes cold and hard.

"Cover your face!" I shouted.

I covered mine and felt Flitz's sharp claws tearing at my hands. Blood flowed down the back of them as his hot breath seared my face.

"Get *off* me!" I cried.

At that moment there was a loud hiccup behind us. Torcher had woken up at last and come to our rescue! He roared angrily, racing across the floor towards Flitz, snapping savagely.

Flitz turned and flew as fast as his wings could take him out through the door again.

"Good old Torcher!" I exclaimed. "You're obviously on the mend!"

There was a fifth charge, and then a sixth. Now Alexandra was getting closer to Dr. Drake and had managed to catch him on the hand with the Spear of Saint George, giving him a nasty wound. Then, as Idraigir turned to fly away from her, Alexandra turned swiftly and stabbed him with a vicious cry.

"Another!" she bellowed.

Dr. Drake faltered as Idraigir lost control beneath him. I watched in horror as the doctor slipped from the saddle and plunged into the water of the lake far below. There was a pause as Idraigir fell to earth with a crash and lay still near the lake edge.

Alexandra whooped.

"One old fool down!" she cried. "Now for the other!"

Her remaining dragons wheeled round again, ready for another attack. But this time, apart from one or two protecting their flanks and another fending off the gargouilles above, they all concentrated on one man: the Master of Hong Wei. I did not think he had a chance. Indeed, although Panthéon and the few remaining uninjured gargouilles did their best to protect him, Alexandra soon managed to stab his dragon, the great Lung Wei, the noble Dragon King of the Western Mountains, deeply in the side with the magical spear. But as he began to fall out of the sky, the Master twisted up and round, grabbing Alexandra and pulling her off her dragon, so that she fell with him down, down into the lake and, heavy with armour, disappeared along with him beneath the surface.

All was quiet. The remaining mahouts did not seem to know what to do without their mistress. Shadwell, who had spent most of his time avoiding the action, now became the leader in a sudden retreat. As Uwassa, Faki-Kifa-Kafi and the others redoubled their counter-attacks in the air, the retreat turned into a panicked rout.

Suddenly Alexandra Gorynytchka, Dr. Drake and the Master erupted out of the water. Dr. Drake, who was bleeding badly, was trying his best to wrestle the end of the Spear of Saint George from Alexandra's grip, while supporting the Master, who was obviously badly hurt, with his other arm. But Alexandra, who was younger and stronger and had sustained no obvious injury, easily wrenched the spear back and swam ashore.

By now Shadwell and the other dragon mahouts, cowed by their defeat, were rapidly disappearing into the distance.

Alexandra looked up at them and raised the Spear of Saint George above her head. "Cowards!" she called, her voice full of rage. "Come back and fight!" The dragon monks surrounded her on every side, but she kept them at bay with the spear.

Dr. Drake climbed, dripping, out of the lake and stepped towards her. "Put down that spear, Miss

Gorynytchka," he said. "The battle is over."

Alexandra laughed. "Surrender to you, Drake?" she cried. "Never!"

"Come now, you must realise that your plan to dominate all dragons is doomed to failure," said Dr. Drake.

"It is the dragons who are doomed," cried Alexandra. "Unless a cure can be found for the dragon plague."

"Then you will be happy to know that a cure has been found," said Dr. Drake. "The Cook children have discovered it."

"Then let those brats beware," said Alexandra, stepping backwards along the shore away from the doctor. "For they have crossed me too many times — as have you! And I am not a woman to be trifled with, believe me! Your old friend Ebenezer Crook would testify to that — if he were alive, of course!"

"Ebenezer Crook!" cried Dr. Drake. "The old Dragon Master! What do you know of him?"

"Aha! So you don't know everything, after all, Ernest," crowed Alexandra, looking over her shoulder towards the cliff edge. "So Ebenezer never told you the story of how he took a keen young dragonologist from Russia as his apprentice, did he?" said Alexandra.

"The keenest student that he ever taught! If Lord Chiddingfold and the rest of the idiots at your so-called Dragonological Society had not insisted that he choose a *British* Dragon Master, he would have made me his successor. He taught me a great many secrets, but he would not let me see his precious treasures — so I stole his vial of black powder and betrayed him!"

"I find it hard to believe that he would ever have chosen *you* as his successor," said Dr. Drake, visibly shocked

"Ah, but you are bitter because he did not like your *dragon science*," said Alexandra, brandishing the spear in the doctor's face. "He did not like the way you spoke of 'dragonology', nor that you wanted to *write* about it in *books*!"

"He changed his mind before the end," said Dr. Drake. "He warned me that a great threat to dragons was coming. I did not know he was warning me about you."

"Ebenezer changed his mind only when he learned of the dragon sickness," said Alexandra. "But until he heard from the Maharawal, he still did not wish to believe that it had been me who stole the vial. He even suspected his own son, Ignatius!"

"Another man who has fallen under your spell," said

Dr. Drake, advancing now, with dragons on either side, so that Alexandra was trapped against the edge of the waterfall.

"Of course he did!" said Alexandra. "And he served me well, for a while. But I tired of him. The stupid fool has gone to find the Lost Isle of Dragons. That's where the vial of black powder was stolen from in the first place. Idiot! He will never succeed without my help."

"Maybe," said Dr. Drake, stepping towards her, the dragons growling menacingly. "Now, put down the spear."

Alexandra laughed. "Enough of this idle chit-chat," she said, twirling the spear in front of her. "It is time for us to part, dear doctor!"

And, before Dr. Drake could do anything, Alexandra gave a last cackle, did a remarkably athletic backflip, and disappeared over the sheer edge of the cliff.

For a moment, everyone was rooted to the spot in amazement, then Dr. Drake ran towards the edge of the cliff and looked over it.

"Can you see her?" exclaimed Beatrice.

"No," said Dr. Drake. "From here, the only way is a sheer drop down."

✳

The battle was over. Hong Wei Temple was saved. We counted our losses. Among the many injured, we had lost five *lung*, including the mighty dragon king Lung Wei, two monks, one war dragon and two of Panthéon's gargouilles. From Alexandra's side, we had captured fifteen mahouts and managed to free sixteen Tunguska war dragons. It was a success, of sorts.

"Their deeds in the service of dragons and humans alike will not go unremembered," said Dr. Drake.

We nodded our heads in agreement.

But of Alexandra Gorynytchka, there was no sign. And although search parties were sent to the bottom of the cliff to recover her body, it was never found.

"She has escaped us," said Dr. Drake. "For the second time. And mark my words: she will be back."

Epilogue
THE CURE

The funeral of Lung Wei, the Dragon King of the Western Mountains, and of the other noble *lung*, monks and gargouilles that had died in the defence of Hong Wei, lasted three days. *Lung* came from all over China to attend, and a huge line of people who held dragons dear snaked up the mountainside to pay their respects to the Dragon King and his faithful allies. Meanwhile, Panthéon and the gargouilles erected a pavilion over their dead comrades and held a motionless vigil for three long nights of remembrance.

"Heaven smiles on these brave creatures who gave their lives to protect ours and those of countless dragons the world over," said the Master of Hong Wei as the *lung* carried away their king's body, to be buried among the floating islands that can sometimes be seen off the coast of China.

"Indeed," said Dr. Drake. "Let them forever inspire

future dragonologists to hold fast to the belief that, above all, dragons must be free."

At that, a roar went up from the dragons, a loud shout of assent arose from the humans and even heroic little Torcher, who was by now back to his old hiccuppy self, sent a long blast of flame skywards.

We spent most of the remainder of our time at Hong Wei administering the cure. Monks had been sent out far and wide to gather up fresh ingredients, and now they worked day and night to make more of the cure. They even commissioned local goldsmiths to make more chalices, so that the process could be speeded up. At last, it was time for us to leave. Uwassa, Idraigir, Panthéon and Faki-Kifa-Kafi had flown home immediately after the funeral, but Dr. Drake had decided that we humans should travel by a more sedate means. So our plan was to sail down a local river to the sea and then take a junk, belonging to Miss Ta's uncle, across the South China Sea and the Indian and Atlantic Oceans back to England. I was quite looking forward to the trip.

On our last night at Hong Wei Temple, Beatrice and I sat looking out over the misty valley with our mother and father. Torcher was sitting next to us, playing with some gems.

"It will be nice to go home," said Beatrice, "and be a proper family again, won't it?"

"Oh, yes," said my mother. "Although, after all your adventures, I do hope you children won't be bored."

"We'll still have Torcher to look after, though, won't we?" I said.

"And he's bound to provide you with all sorts of amusement," said my father. "You will still continue to study dragonology, after all. Speaking of which, in commemoration of your voyage on the Dragon Express, Dr. Drake has asked your mother and me to give you a rather special gift. You are each to receive a dragon whistle as a mark of the fact that you are being promoted to Dragonologists Second Class! Well done!"

"The whistles have been prepared by the Master of Hong Wei himself," said my mother. "They are made of jade and precious metals. You can blow different sounds on them to summon different sorts of dragon. Have you got them, John?"

But my father's face had fallen. He was patting his pockets.

"I had them here a minute ago," he said.

"You, er, didn't show them to a certain dragon chick, did you?" I said. "Because for some reason, Torcher has disappeared..."

DR. ERNEST DRAKE

The existence of remarkable Victorian dragonologist Dr. Ernest Drake first came to light with the alleged discovery of a book simply entitled *Dragonology* in early 2003. This volume, a natural history book with the central theme of dragons, was supposedly the sole survivor of a print run of only one hundred copies. It was particularly interesting in its treatment of dragons as actual, living animals rather than the mythological creatures they had hitherto been supposed to be. The one remaining copy was said to have been found in an old shop near the Seven Dials in London, not far from where Dr. Drake's Dragonalia itself must have stood. *Dragonology* was edited by the current author and published in facsimile form, to some acclaim. Since then, further works by Dr. Drake have come to light and have been similarly published.

The author's diligent researches into Dr. Drake and his life both in London and in St. Leonard's Forest in Sussex have proved as fruitful as they are ongoing. However, rather than simply write Dr. Drake's life in a dry, bibliographical fashion, the author determined to write the story of Dr. Drake and the S.A.S.D. from the point of view of one of the people who came to know him best of all, his dragonological apprentice, Daniel Cook. In this way, the author hopes to convey a sense of what it would really have been like to have studied dragons, and dragonology, with Ernest Drake, in addition to recounting some of the most important events ever to take place in either the world of the dragons themselves, or in the history of the Secret and Ancient Society of Dragonologists.

One thing is certain: As further facts emerge about Dr. Drake and his tireless work in the conservation and protection of dragons, they are sure to be revealed.

Dugald A. Steer, London

THE SAGA CONTINUES…

Watch out for the next exciting instalment of Beatrice and Daniel's adventures!

THE DRAGON'S APPRENTICE

Vol. III

Coming soon from Templar Publishing

PRAISE FOR *DRAGONOLOGY*

"... an extraordinary and unusual book, wonderfully indulgent – and equally accessible to children and adults."
Publishing News, Tony West of Lion and Unicorn Bookshop

"... a striking object... It is a book to pore over and savour for its painstaking details and its jokes."
Sunday Times

"This is more than one expects from a book – it's a total experience... readers will spend many afternoons engrossed in the gorgeous art and sophisticated language of Dugald Steer's book."
The Children's Literature Program

"Anyone wanting to find out more about dragons should rush to buy Dr. Ernest Drake's Dragonology... *I revelled in it and so did my children."*
The Times

"A fine example of what a fertile imagination can do when allowed to soar."
Judges of Oppenheim Toy Portfolio Gold Award